Learning QlikView Data Visualization

Visualize and analyze data with the most intuitive business intelligence tool, QlikView

Karl Pover

BIRMINGHAM - MUMBAI

Learning QlikView Data Visualization

Copyright © 2013 Packt Publishing

All rights reserved. No part of this book may be reproduced, stored in a retrieval system, or transmitted in any form or by any means, without the prior written permission of the publisher, except in the case of brief quotations embedded in critical articles or reviews.

Every effort has been made in the preparation of this book to ensure the accuracy of the information presented. However, the information contained in this book is sold without warranty, either express or implied. Neither the author, nor Packt Publishing, and its dealers and distributors will be held liable for any damages caused or alleged to be caused directly or indirectly by this book.

Packt Publishing has endeavored to provide trademark information about all of the companies and products mentioned in this book by the appropriate use of capitals. However, Packt Publishing cannot guarantee the accuracy of this information.

First published: September 2013

Production Reference: 1190913

Published by Packt Publishing Ltd.
Livery Place
35 Livery Street
Birmingham B3 2PB, UK.

ISBN 978-1-78217-989-4

www.packtpub.com

Cover Image by Jarek Blaminsky (milak6@wp.pl)

Credits

Author
Karl Pover

Reviewers
Ralf Becher
Winnie Yu

Acquisition Editor
Kartikey Pandey
Rebecca Youe

Commissioning Editor
Mohammed Fahad

Technical Editors
Sandeep Madnaik
Shali Sasidharan

Project Coordinator
Suraj Bist

Proofreaders
Amy Johnson
Hardip Sidhu

Indexer
Rekha Nair

Graphics
Yuvraj Mannari

Production Coordinator
Melwyn D'sa

Cover Work
Melwyn D'sa

Foreword

If you are holding this book in your hands, chances are that you know a thing or two about QlikView. And if you have experienced QlikView at least a little bit, you are probably just as amazed by it as most of us QlikView professionals. People often wonder what makes QlikView so attractive and fascinating. I can offer my own version of an explanation.

In our complex and hectic world, QlikView offers SIMPLICITY. In our world of multi-volume operational manuals, endless regulations, processes and procedures, service-level agreements, and software development life cycles, QlikView is like a sip of cold sparkling water on a hot summer afternoon. It's like playing a video game while everybody else around is working hard.

This abundant simplicity makes QlikView a perfect tool for people in business that would otherwise never consider themselves to be application developers. This includes business analysts, managers, supply chain professionals, credit analysts, and other business people, hungry for information and happy to get access to it in such a simple way.

Simplicity shouldn't, however, be mistaken for plainness. Despite the ease of use, QlikView has a lot of depth. And ease of use shouldn't be mistaken for illiteracy. You still need to know what you are doing in order to produce a worthy analysis.

That is why this book will provide tremendous value to huge masses of business analysts that have the opportunity to use QlikView in their jobs, and want to get the most out of it. It will teach people how to leverage QlikView's simplicity to produce insightful visualizations.

When I first heard that Karl Pover had written a book about QlikView visualizations, I thought to myself "Oh, no! Not another QlikView book for beginners.". In the last few years, a number of QlikView books for beginners have been published, some better than others (I personally recommend *QlikVew 11 for Developers*, *Barry Harmsen* and *Mike Garcia*, and *QlikView 11 for Developers Cookbook*, *Stephen Redmond*). So, at that point, I clearly couldn't see the value of another beginners' book. However, after I read the final draft, I realized that this book is very different. It has a different purpose and a different audience. Most other QlikView books teach QlikView. This book teaches how to build effective visualizations using QlikView. In other words, instead of teaching you properties of a scatter chart, this book will first teach you what type of analysis require a scatter chart before going on to instruct you how to put one together in QlikView and make its presentation meaningful and professional.

The author, Karl Pover, is an excellent educator and practitioner. He sharpened his pencil on QlikCommunity, the forum of QlikView professionals where thousands of QlikView developers share knowledge and help each other grow. Karl and I first met there, in the tight group of Top 10 Contributors. Karl was helping hundreds of new developers with his technical advice. For many of the active QlikCommunity contributors, answering hundreds of questions was the best way of learning the deepest layers of QlikView's functionality.

As one of the first QlikView consultants in Mexico, Karl has a passion for improving the quality of QlikView services, coupled with his keen sense of design and presentation. Karl's work in QlikView and this book is clearly influenced by Stephen Few and Edward Tufte, the two gurus that have shaped the industry standards of data visualization.

In *Learning QlikView Data Visualization*, Karl Pover describes several common types of analysis, along with the best practices of data visualization. He then combines this with the technical workflow of configuring them in QlikView and boils it all down to a simple recipe. For example, this is how you do trend analysis in QlikView, and this is how you improve it to make it more meaningful.

This book is fast and intense. In about a hundred pages, it will teach you the basics of building effective visualizations in QlikView, and will leave you with the desire to learn more.

Oleg Troyansky
President
Natural Synergies, Inc.

About the Author

Karl Pover is co-owner of Evolution Consulting (`http://www.evolcon.com`), which provides QlikView consulting services throughout Mexico. Since 2006, he has been dedicated to providing QlikView pre-sales, implementation, training, and expert services. He has worked in more than 50 companies and government agencies, and set up QlikView competence centers that expand the globe. Most importantly, he has formed a team of highly capable consultants that together have done far more than him.

Recently, he has started a blog (`http://www.poverconsulting.com`) that will continue to share his experiences in the world of data discovery.

I couldn't have written this book without the loving support and patience of my wife, Pamela.

I would also like to thank the consulting team at Evolution Consulting, especially my business partner, José Angel, and the founding consultants, Carlos and Julian, for their excellent work day in, day out.

Thanks to my old boss, John, for introducing me to QlikView back in 2006.

Finally, thanks to my family, and my friend, Eric, for giving me a shot of confidence and my dog, Axel, for keeping me company during those long nights of writing and revising.

About the Reviewers

Ralf Becher worked as an IT system architect and as an IT consultant since 1989 in the areas of banking, insurance, logistics, automotive, and retail. He founded TIQ Solutions in 2004 with partners.

The Leipzig company specializes in modern, quality-assured data management. Since 2004 it has been helping its customers process, evaluate and maintain the quality of company data, helping them introduce, implement, and improve complex solutions in the fields of data architecture, data integration, data migration, master data management, meta-data management, data warehousing, and business intelligence.

He is an internationally recognized QlikView expert with a strong position in the QlikCommunity. He started working with QlikView in 2006 and has contributed QlikView add-on solutions for data quality and data integration, especially for connectivity in the Java and Big Data realm. He runs his QlikView data integration blog at `http://tiqview.tumblr.com/`.

Winnie Yu graduated from the City University of New York, Baruch College in 2006 and after formal training in QlikView, she has been developing and designing applications in QlikView for a few years.

She will continue to deliver business intelligence solutions through the use of QlikView because of her enthusiasm for it and the ability it brings to users to allow them to analyze their data to make appropriate business decisions within a short amount of time.

www.PacktPub.com

Support files, eBooks, discount offers and more

You might want to visit www.PacktPub.com for support files and downloads related to your book.

Did you know that Packt offers eBook versions of every book published, with PDF and ePub files available? You can upgrade to the eBook version at www.PacktPub.com and as a print book customer, you are entitled to a discount on the eBook copy. Get in touch with us at service@packtpub.com for more details.

At www.PacktPub.com, you can also read a collection of free technical articles, sign up for a range of free newsletters and receive exclusive discounts and offers on Packt books and eBooks.

http://PacktLib.PacktPub.com

Do you need instant solutions to your IT questions? PacktLib is Packt's online digital book library. Here, you can access, read and search across Packt's entire library of books.

Why Subscribe?

- Fully searchable across every book published by Packt
- Copy and paste, print and bookmark content
- On demand and accessible via web browser

Free Access for Packt account holders

If you have an account with Packt at www.PacktPub.com, you can use this to access PacktLib today and view nine entirely free books. Simply use your login credentials for immediate access.

Instant Updates on New Packt Books

Get notified! Find out when new books are published by following @PacktEnterprise on Twitter, or the *Packt Enterprise* Facebook page.

Table of Contents

Preface

Data visualization is a powerful analytical technique and an exciting form of communication. Only in the past few decades has the advent of the personal computer helped it become a more widely used method to explain events, investigate cause-effect relationships, and search for opportunities among growing amounts data.

Data visualization has come a long way since being used solely as eye-candy on top of tabular spreadsheets. Slowly, but surely, we are coming to realize that flashy 3-dimensional charts are neither evidence of a particular software's effectiveness nor of a well-executed analysis. Instead of glitzy graphs, we are now looking for ways to quickly and easily create insightful data visualizations in software that complements our thought processes.

QlikView has been that software for thousands of empowered business users. The ability to rapidly produce powerful analysis and data visualization on top of a data model developed to imitate human thought has placed QlikView at the vanguard of data discovery tools.

QlikView lends the responsibility of choosing the most suitable data visualizations to us. In real world implementations, the freedom to choose how data is visualized has minimized the resistance to the change brought on by migrating old, static corporate reports, and spreadsheets to a new platform. However, we need to grow and learn how to create the best data visualization that allows us to fully benefit from QlikView's dynamism.

In the following chapters, we propose a data visualization style guide and apply it to various forms of analysis in QlikView. We will not cover all of the software's available visualization options, but rather we review a selected mix of both basic and advanced functions that covers the most valuable analytical techniques.

We pack as much content as possible into as few pages as possible to give you a quick return on your investment of time and money. The book is written to be read from start to finish, and then, used as a reference book for your own data discovery experience. We hope this book is part of a continual learning process to create great data visualization with QlikView.

What this book covers

Chapter1, First Things First, explains how finding the right people, data, and tools is key to creating great data visualizations. Finally, we start our first exercise in data discovery.

Chapter 2, Rank Analysis, explains how to use bar charts to create analysis that ranks values. We introduce the data visualization style guide.

Chapter3, Trend Analysis, helps us discover how line charts show us how our company has changed over time.

Chapter4, Multivariate Analysis, explains ways to analyze a large amount of variables using straight and pivot tables along with heat maps.

Chapter5, Distribution Analysis and Statistics, takes our analysis further by adding more sophisticated statistical analysis. We review the histogram, frequency polygon, and box plot chart.

Chapter6, Correlation Analysis, looks for relationships between variables using scatterplot charts.

Chapter7, Geographical Analysis, brings to light how location adds insightful information with a geographical chart. We introduce the use of extensions.

Chapter8, What-if Analysis, explains how to include variables that we can change to create possible future scenarios.

Chapter9, Dashboard and Navigation, brings everything together to communicate the results of our analysis. In the process, we propose a solution and create a way to monitor its execution.

What you need for this book

You will need a computer and internet access to download QlikView and additional files required to perform the exercises throughout the book. Download the additional files in the **Support** section of `http://www.packtpub.com/learning-qlikview-data-visualization/book`. If you are using the QlikView Personal Edition, follow the instructions included in downloaded files before starting the exercises.

Who this book is for

This book is for anybody interested in performing powerful data analysis and crafting insightful data visualization independent of their previous knowledge of QlikView.

Conventions

In this book, you will find a number of styles of text that distinguish between different kinds of information. Here are some examples of these styles, and an explanation of their meaning.

Code words in text are shown as follows: "The resulting expression is `Sum ([Net Sales])`."

A block of code is set as follows:

```
if(Division='Government',Blue(200),RGB(150,150,150))
```

New terms and **important words** are shown in bold. Words that you see on the screen, in menus or dialog boxes for example, appear in the text like this: "Right-click on the new chart and select **Properties...**"

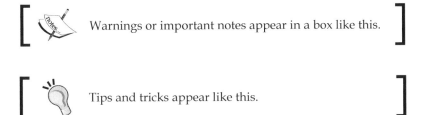

Warnings or important notes appear in a box like this.

Tips and tricks appear like this.

Reader feedback

Feedback from our readers is always welcome. Let us know what you think about this book—what you liked or may have disliked. Reader feedback is important for us to develop titles that you really get the most out of.

To send us general feedback, simply send an e-mail to `feedback@packtpub.com`, and mention the book title via the subject of your message.

If there is a topic that you have expertise in and you are interested in either writing or contributing to a book, see our author guide on `www.packtpub.com/authors`.

Customer support

Now that you are the proud owner of a Packt book, we have a number of things to help you to get the most from your purchase.

Downloading the example code

You can download the example code files for all Packt books you have purchased from your account at http://www.packtpub.com. If you purchased this book elsewhere, you can visit http://www.packtpub.com/support and register to have the files e-mailed directly to you.

Errata

Although we have taken every care to ensure the accuracy of our content, mistakes do happen. If you find a mistake in one of our books—maybe a mistake in the text or the code—we would be grateful if you would report this to us. By doing so, you can save other readers from frustration and help us improve subsequent versions of this book. If you find any errata, please report them by visiting http://www.packtpub.com/submit-errata, selecting your book, clicking on the **erratasubmissionform** link, and entering the details of your errata. Once your errata are verified, your submission will be accepted and the errata will be uploaded on our website, or added to any list of existing errata, under the Errata section of that title. Any existing errata can be viewed by selecting your title from http://www.packtpub.com/support.

Piracy

Piracy of copyright material on the Internet is an ongoing problem across all media. At Packt, we take the protection of our copyright and licenses very seriously. If you come across any illegal copies of our works, in any form, on the Internet, please provide us with the location address or website name immediately so that we can pursue a remedy.

Please contact us at copyright@packtpub.comwith a link to the suspected pirated material.

We appreciate your help in protecting our authors, and our ability to bring you valuable content.

Questions

You can contact us at questions@packtpub.com if you are having a problem with any aspect of the book, and we will do our best to address it.

1
First Things First

We are anxious to start our data visualization project, but if we fail to understand the context within which we are working, we are more prone to make trivial, gaudy graphs. We want to craft great data visualization, and to do this, we first analyze the most important elements of its foundation: **people**, **data**, and **tools**.

Project background

We are data discovery experts who work for QDataViz, Inc. Our fictitious company is extremely successful at helping our customers get the most out of their data using our best practices in data visualization.

However, all is not well for QDataViz, Inc., and our CEO, Charles W. Smith, Jr. has invited us to a meeting to discuss a plan to help the company turn its losses into a profit. In the meeting, Charles remarks that while we are excellent advisors to our customers, we have failed to use our best practices internally to support the decisions of our colleagues.

He entrusts us data discovery experts to review our company's data, and more importantly, to empower our colleagues to perform the analysis necessary to improve the company's situation.

People

People are the only active element of data visualization, and as such, they are the most important. We briefly describe the roles of several people that participate in our project, but we mainly focus on the person who is going to analyze and visualize the data.

After the meeting, we get together with our colleague, Samantha, who is the analyst that supports the sales and executive teams. She currently manages a series of highly personalized Excels that she creates from standard reports generated within the customer invoice and project management system. Her audience ranges from the CEO down to sales managers. She is not a pushover, but she is open to try new techniques, especially given that the sponsor of this project is the CEO of QDataViz, Inc.

As a data discovery user, Samantha possesses the following traits:

Ownership

She has a stake in the project's success or failure. She, along with the company, stands to grow as a result of this project, and most importantly, she is aware of this opportunity.

Driven

She is focused on grasping what we teach her and is self-motivated to continue learning after the project is finished. The cause of her drive is unimportant as long as she remains honest.

Honest

She understands that data is a passive element that is open to diverse interpretations by different people. She resists basing her arguments on deceptive visualization techniques or data omission.

Flexible

She does not endanger her job and company results following every technological fad or whimsical idea. However, she realizes that technology does change and that a new approach can foment breakthroughs.

Analytical

She loves finding anomalies in the data and being the reason that action is taken to improve QDataViz, Inc. As a means to achieve what she loves, she understands how to apply functions and methods to manipulate data.

Knowledgeable

She is familiar with the company's data, and she understands the indicators needed to analyze its performance. Additionally, she serves as a data source and gives context to analysis.

Team player

She respects the roles of her colleagues and holds them accountable. In turn, she demands respect and is also obliged to meet her responsibilities.

Data

Our next meeting involves Samantha and Ivan, our **Information Technology (IT)** Director. While Ivan explains the data available in the customer invoice and project management system's well-defined databases, Samantha adds that she has vital data in Microsoft Excel that is missing from those databases. One Excel file contains the sales budget and another contains an additional customer grouping; both files are necessary to present information to the CEO.

We take advantage of this discussion to highlight the following characteristics that make data easy to analyze.

Reliable

Ivan is going to document the origin of the tables and fields, which increases Samantha's confidence in the data. He is also going to perform a basic data cleansing and eliminate duplicate records whose only difference is a period, two transposed letters, or an abbreviation.

Once the system is operational, Ivan will consider the impact any change in the customer invoice and project management system may have on the data. He will also verify that the data is continually updated while Samantha helps confirm the data's validity.

Detailed

Ivan will preserve as much detail as possible. If he is unable to handle large volumes of data as a whole, he will segment the detailed data by month and reduce the detail of a year's data in a consistent fashion. Conversely, he is will consider adding detail by prorating payments between the products of paid invoices in order to maintain a consistent level of detail between invoices and payments.

Formal

An Excel file as a data source is a short-term solution. While Ivan respects its temporary use to allow for a quick, first release of the data visualization project, he takes responsibility to find a more stable medium to long-term solution. In the span of a few months, he will consider modifying the invoice system, investing in additional software, or creating a simple portal to upload Excel files to a database.

Flexible

Ivan will not prevent progress solely for bureaucratic reasons. Samantha respects that Ivan's goal is to make data more standardized, secure, and recoverable. However, Ivan knows that if he does not move as quickly as business does, he will become irrelevant as Samantha and others create their own black market of company data.

Referential

Ivan is going to make available manifold perspectives of QDataViz, Inc. He will maintain history, budgets, and forecasts by customers, salespersons, divisions, states, and projects. Additionally, he will support segmenting these dimensions into multiple groups, subgroups, classes, and types.

Tools

We continue our meeting with Ivan and Samantha, but we now change our focus to what tool we will use to foster great data visualization and analysis. We create the following list of basic features we hope from this tool:

Fast and easy implementation

We should be able to learn the tool quickly and be able to deliver a first version of our data visualization project within a matter of weeks. In this fashion, we start receiving a return on our investment within a short period of time.

Business empowerment

Samantha should be able to continue her analysis with little help from us. Also, her audience should be able to easily perform their own lightweight analysis and follow up on the decisions made.

Enterprise-ready

Ivan should be able to maintain hundreds or thousands of users and data volumes that exceed 100 million rows. He should also be able to restrict access to certain data to certain users. Finally, he needs to have the confidence that the tools will remain available even if a server fails.

Based on these expectations, we talk about data discovery tools, which are increasingly becoming part of the architecture of many organizations. Samantha can use these tools for self-service data analysis. In other words, she can create her own data visualizations without having to depend on pre-built graphs or reports. At the same time, Ivan can be reassured that the tool does not interfere with his goal of providing an enterprise solution that offers scalability, security, and high availability.

The data discovery tool we are going to use is QlikView, and the following diagram shows the overall architecture we will build and where this book focuses its attention:

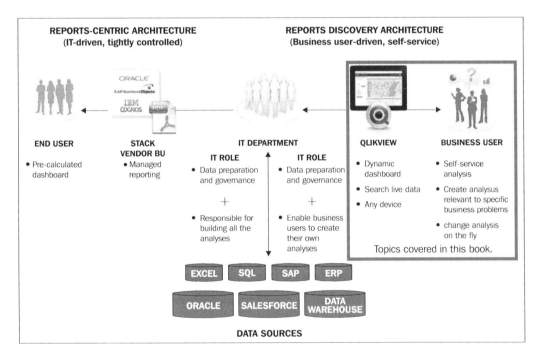

QlikView

There are several data discovery tools on the market and each has its strengths and weaknesses; however, QlikView is arguably the most well-rounded data discovery tool. QlikView provides an all-in-one tool with the ability to extract and transform raw data, construct a data model, and create dynamic data visualizations. It deploys as a departmental or enterprise solution within small, medium, or large organizations.

QlikView's greatest product differentiation is what it calls its **associative data model**. QlikView's associative data model is a type of pervasive filtering. When we filter the values in any field, all the values in every other field, independent of the table it belongs to, will automatically be filtered according to their direct or indirect relationship with the values we filtered. Since this is an intensive process, all the data is compressed and stored in a computer's RAM memory.

Along with facilitating development and accelerating deployment, this feature aids our own analytical process. We can only think about one topic in detail for so long before asking questions about a related topic. In our QlikView application, Samantha will easily dig deep into our sales data and analyze it by salesperson and customer, and then, upon finding something interesting, change the perspective to look at sales and costs by project. Finally, she will end up comparing the consultants' real costs against estimated costs, first in particular projects, and then in all projects. Astoundingly, all this will happen with ease in the same data model within one QlikView application.

Once Samantha has concluded her robust analysis, she will use QlikView to present her diagnosis of QDataViz, Inc.'s problems and allow users to interact with her supporting analysis. For this reason, we consider QlikView our tool to develop ideas, test theories, and communicate our conclusions to a critical, participating audience.

Installing QlikView

Samantha is new to QlikView so we are going to show her how to install the software in her computer. First, we go to `http://download.qlikview.com`, register a user, and then download QlikView Desktop. In this project, we will be using version 11. We install QlikView following a very simple installation wizard, and request a named license from the IT department for this project. (If you don't have a named license, please follow the instructions included in the book's exercise files.)

Downloading the example code

You can download the example code files for all Packt books you have purchased from your account at http://www.packtpub.com. If you purchased this book elsewhere, you can visit http://www.packtpub.com/support and register to have the files e-mailed directly to you.

Important general configuration

Before we load the data, it is important to perform the following tasks:

1. Open QlikView.

2. Right-click over the existing toolbars and select **Design** to show the design toolbar.

3. In the design toolbar, click on User Preferences and select the **Save Before Reload** checkbox located in the **Save** tab.

Now we are ready to open our first QlikView application.

Let's start discovering data

We are going to start our business discovery process by first opening a QlikView application and then taking a look at the data model and its metadata. Finally, we will preview the data directly in the data model before creating our first QlikView objects.

Opening our first QlikView application

Having read "QlikView 11 for Developers", Ivan has prepared a QlikView application with QDataViz, Inc.'s customer invoice and project management data.

Let's open the QlikView application.

1. Click on Open in the standard toolbar.

2. Browse for the Exercises\Original\ folder and open Sales_Project_Analysis_Sandbox.qvw.

Once the QlikView application opens, we notice an empty sheet where Samantha is going to play with the data, creating and destroying objects as if it were an analyst's sandbox.

A QlikView application contains a snapshot of past data. Anytime we want to update the data, we click on Reload in the standard toolbar.

Data model

In our QlikView application, click on Table Viewer at the end of the design toolbar to preview the data model. The data model looks similar to the following screenshot:

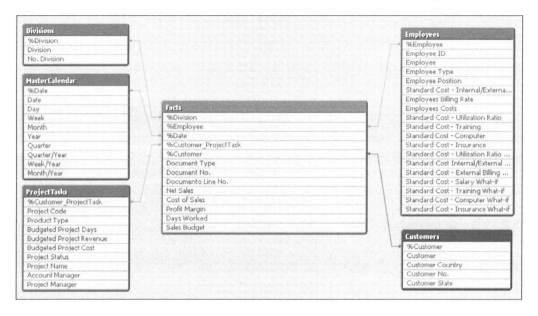

Ivan has created the invoices and project management data model based on the star schema. We prefer to use the star schema because it facilitates analysis. The numeric values of an event are stored in one central fact table while related descriptive data is grouped into surrounding dimension tables.

Metadata

Metadata is data that describes data. Among other things, metadata includes descriptions of data volume, age, source, and usage. In our QlikView application, we are interested in information that explains what kind of data we can expect to find in our data model.

Metadata is not a necessary component of QlikView. However, since our goal is to empower business users, Ivan has included table and field descriptions in our data model. Alongside user-friendly table and field names, this accelerates our data discovery experience. We can see the metadata in the same Table Viewer window by hovering over any table or field as shown in the following screenshot:

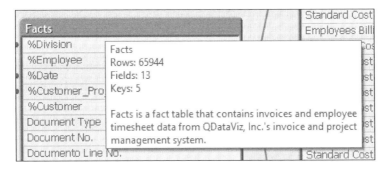

Data preview

Finally, we can go further and preview the actual data in the model by right-clicking on any table and selecting **Preview**. QlikView displays a 1000-row preview of the data. A cell that contains a dash (-) means that the value is null, or that data does not exist for that cell.

Listboxes

Listboxes are the easiest and most powerful way to perform an initial discovery of our data. Listboxes are lists of all the unique values in a field. Its behavior as we filter values can help us answer many questions about our data.

For example, Samantha's first task is to validate the quality of the data. She starts by investigating how well the invoices and projects are defined by division.

We find our answer by carrying out the following steps:

1. Right-click on the blank sheet and click on **Select Fields...**

2. In the **Show Fields from Table** drop-down box, select **Divisions**. In the above list of fields, select **No. Division** and **Division** and then click on **Add >**.

3. In the **Show Fields from Table** drop-down box, select **Customers**. In the above list of fields, select **No. Customer** and **Customer** and then click on **Add >**.

4. In the **Show Fields from Table** drop-down box, select **ProjectTasks**. In the above list of fields, select **Project Code** and **Project Name** and then click on **Add >**.

5. In the **Show Fields from Table** drop-down box, select **MasterCalendar**. In the above list of fields, select **Year** and **Month** and then click on **Add >**.

6. In the **Show Fields from Table** drop-down box, select **Facts**. In the above list of fields, select **Net Sales** and then click on **Add >**.

7. Click on **OK**.

8. Move the listboxes by clicking on their captions and dragging them to anywhere on the sheet.

Among the available values in the listbox containing QDataViz, Inc.'s divisions, we notice the value **N/A,** which indicates that several transactions may exist that have not been assigned a division. Let's select **N/A** and analyze the results that are shown in the following screenshot:

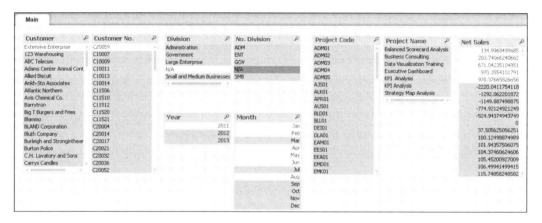

Based on the selection made in the screenshot, we discover that during the year 2011, several transactions for the customer Extensive Enterprise were not assigned to any project. The transactions occurred during multiple months, but luckily the net sales amounts appears to be small.

We are able to come to this conclusion because QlikView listboxes use the color scheme shown in the following screenshot when filtering its values:

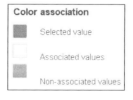

Table boxes

An alternative to a series of listboxes is a table box. Table boxes show us unique rows of related data from one or more tables.

Let's create a table box containing the fact table fields with the following steps:

1. Click on Create Table Box ⊞ in the design toolbar.
2. Clear the **Show System Fields** checkbox.
3. In the **Show Fields from Table** drop-down box, select **Facts**.
4. Click on **Add All >**.
5. In the **Presentation** tab, select all the values in the **Fields** list.
6. Select the **Dropdown Select** checkbox.
7. Click on **OK**.

The resulting table shown in the following screenshot displays each document that is associated with the division **N/A**:

We observe that several documents are not assigned to a proper division. Although Samantha will work with Ivan to clean up each transaction, we conclude that the unassigned amounts are relatively small and do not prevent us from continuing our analysis of QDataViz, Inc.'s data.

We repeat the above process a hundred times over as new questions arise about our data. In this way, we take advantage of QlikView's flexibility to easily and quickly discover data.

Before moving on to rank analysis, we save our QlikView application with the following step:

1. Click on Save in the standard toolbar.

Summary

People, data, and tools are an essential part of creating great data visualization and analysis. We are going to provide Samantha with the power of self-service data discovery using QlikView over our customer invoice and project management data.

We briefly covered how to open a QlikView application and review its data model. Also, we learned the color scheme QlikView uses to filter data and how to create listboxes and table boxes to perform basic data discovery and test the quality of our data.

In the following chapter, we will learn how to use rank analysis to concentrate our efforts on finding problems that have the most effect on QDataViz, Inc.'s performance.

2
Rank Analysis

Who are our most important customers? What are our most important products or services? These inquiries are usually the first made by any company. The answer is essential because it helps the company focus on what has the most effect on its health.

What is rank analysis?

Rank analysis is the most basic analysis. We simply want to know who did the most or least of something. Samantha's first task is to find QDataViz, Inc.'s top-selling customers. This is important because the return on investment of the hours spent analyzing our best customer's detailed data is greater than if we had to sift through the detailed data of every customer.

Rank analysis can be done in a variety of ways. In the case of finding the top-selling customers, we can choose to show an arbitrary number of customers, customers that buy more than an arbitrary percentage of total company sales, or customers that compose an arbitrary percentage of total company sales.

There is no right answer. That is why we created a QlikView sandbox application that will allow Samantha to play with the data. For example, she may choose to show the ten top-selling customers, customers that have bought more than five percent of total company sales or customers that compose eighty percent of total company sales.

What is certain is that we will use a bar chart to do rank analysis.

Bar chart

Let's create a new sheet and then a bar chart to analyze the ranking of our top-selling customers with the following steps:

1. Open the QlikView application, `Sales_Project_Analysis_Sandbox.qvw`.

2. Click on Add Sheet in the design toolbar.

3. Click on Sheet Properties in the design toolbar.

4. In the **General** tab, type `Rank Analysis` into the **Title** textbox.

5. Click on **OK**.

6. Click on Create Chart in the design toolbar. In the Create Chart wizard, we consider the following three steps when creating the following chart:

1. Choose the type of chart desired. Since the bar chart (shown in the previous image) is selected by default, click on **Next>**.

2. Choose a dimension that groups the metric defined in the next step. Since we want to see sales by customer, the dimension is customer. So, in the **Available Fields/Groups** list on the left side of the window, select **Customer**, click on **Add>**, and then click on **Next>**.

3. Define a metric, or an expression. Again, since we want to see sales by customer, the metric is the sum of the sales. So, in the **Edit Expression** window, select **Sum** within the **Aggregation** drop-down box, **Facts** within the **Table** drop-down box, and **Net Sales** within the **Field** drop-down box. Click on **Paste**. The resulting expression is `Sum ([Net Sales])`. Click on **OK** and then click on **Finish**.

> Field names in QlikView are case-sensitive and are surrounded by square brackets ([]) when the field name contains a space or a special character such as the forward slash (/). QlikView functions are not case-sensitive.

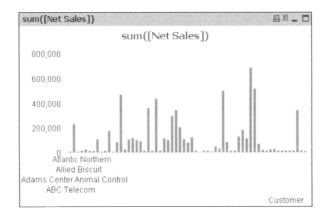

Now, let's see how to modify the bar chart to display a rank analysis using the following steps:

1. Right-click on the chart object and select **Properties...**

2. In the **Sort** tab, select the **Y-value** checkbox and verify that **Descending** is selected in the drop-down box to the right.

 The **Y-value** is the first metric listed in the **Expressions** tab. In this case, the chart sorts customers by their corresponding sum of net sales, or Sum ([Net Sales]).

3. In the **Presentation** tab, select the **Enable X-Axis Scrollbar** checkbox and leave the default value of 10 in the **When Number of Items Exceeds:** textbox. This allows us to only view a maximum of 10 customers at one time.

4. Click on **OK**.

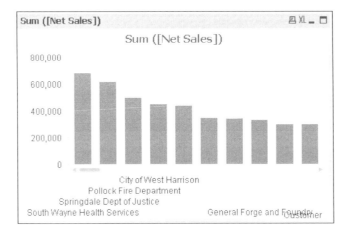

At this point in time, we barely understand the resulting bar chart as shown in the previous screenshot, but before reviewing the data visualization style guide for bar charts, let's add a few supporting objects.

Objects to support bar charts

The listbox, search object, and current selections box add value to our rank analysis.

Listbox

In the same fashion we created listboxes in the previous chapter; we add listboxes of **Month**, **Year**, **Division**, and **Product Type** to the **Rank Analysis** sheet and place them on the left side of the sheet.

Search object

Just like a search engine, we can look for any value in the data model using a search object by performing the following steps:

1. Click on Create Search Object  in the design toolbar.
2. Click on **OK**.

Current selections box

As we filter different fields, the current selections box keeps track of every filter that is currently applied. We use its information to correctly interpret the charts we are viewing. This is done with the following steps:

1. Click on Create Current Selections box 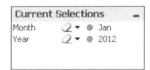 in the design toolbar.
2. Click on **OK**.

Now, let's propose a data visualization style guide that contains a set of rules for effective analysis and communication.

Data visualization style guide for bar charts

A data visualization style guide is a set of rules aimed to increase a chart's data density while at the same time respecting usability. Each chart type has its particular rules and we will revisit this style guide for each chart type. First, let's look at the guide for bar charts.

Rule 1 – use adequate labeling

Each component of a chart should be correctly labeled and understandable. We use **Tahoma** as the font for all labels. The font size ranges between **8** and **10**.

Chart labels

The first label should inform the chart's intent to the audience. Follow these steps:

1. Right-click on the chart object and select **Properties...**
2. In the **General** tab, type `Top-selling customers based on net sales` into the **Window Title** textbox.
3. Clear the **Show Title in Chart** checkbox.
4. In the **Caption** tab, click **Font...** and select the font **Tahoma** and size **10**.
5. Click on **OK** twice.

In some cases, we may favor hiding the caption and choosing to show the title in the chart. However, we resist hiding captions for the following reasons:

- The caption contains useful shortcuts (for example, export to Excel, maximize, and help.)
- The caption's text is visible if the object is minimized or within a container.

Dimension and metric labels

The next labels describe each bar:

1. Right-click on the chart object and select **Properties...**

 We recommend naming fields in the data model as we would like to label them in our charts.

2. In the **Dimensions** tab, we leave the **Label** textbox blank because the field's name, **Customer**, is adequate.

3. In the **Style** tab, click on **Horizontal Orientation** (shown in the previous image) in the **Orientation** section.

4. Click on **OK**.

We prefer horizontal bar charts over vertical bar charts for the following reasons:

- The bars' labels in a horizontal bar chart are easier to read since most cultures naturally read left to right, or right to left

- The bars' labels in a horizontal bar chart handle longer descriptions.

We use vertical bar charts when the dimension is time-based or occasionally when the bars' descriptions don't exceed ten characters.

Metric labels appear in legends when more than one metric is defined or in the pop-up that is shown when we hover over a bar. We add metric labels using the following steps:

1. Right-click on the chart object and select **Properties...**

2. In the **Expression** tab, type `Net Sales` in the **Label** textbox.

3. Optionally, select the **Values on Data Points** checkbox to display the numeric values of the metric to the right of each bar.

4. Click on **OK**.

Axes labels

The final labels we define are the axes labels. We add labels to the axes with the following steps:

1. Right-click on the chart object and select **Properties...**

2. In the **Number** tab, select **Integer**.

3. Further down in the same tab, type $ in the **Symbol** textbox, $K in the **Thousand Symbol** textbox, and $M in the **Million Symbol** textbox.
   This label appears in the metric, expression, or axis.

4. In the **Axes** tab, click on **Font...** in the **Expression Axes** section, and select font **Tahoma** and size **8**. Click on **OK**.

5. In the same tab, click on **Font...** in the **Dimension Axes** section, and select font **Tahoma** and size **8**. Click on **OK**.

6. Click on **OK**.

The thousands, millions, and billions unit labels only affect the axis. The underlying metric values remain unchanged. If we want the value of the metric to be in thousands or millions, we divide the expression by 1,000. For example, Sum ([Net Sales])/1000.

We now have a clear, simple rank analysis as shown in the following image:

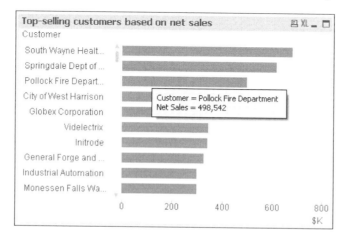

Rule 2 – convert color into data

We resist adding color just to make charts flashier. We lose a great opportunity to add insightful data if we color each bar differently, or use a corporate color scheme for no other reason than to make it pretty. We propose four effective coloring techniques for bar charts: associative, highlighting, alerts, and heat map.

Associative

The associative coloring technique is useful when the dimension has less than ten values. A certain color is assigned to each value so that we can associate different data between various juxtaposed charts that use the same dimension.

Let's clone the current graph, and then apply the associative coloring technique using the following steps:

1. Right-click on the chart **Top-selling customers based on net sales** and select **Clone**.

2. Drag the new chart object away from the original chart object.

3. Right-click on the new chart and select **Properties...**

4. In the **General** tab, change the caption title to `Top-selling customers based on net sales (Associative)`.

5. In the **Colors** tab, select both the **Mulitcolored** and **Persistent Colors** checkboxes.

6. Optionally, in the upper left-hand corner of the same tab, change the available colors used for the bars.

7. Click on **OK**.

Repeat the same procedure for the juxtaposed charts that use the same dimension.

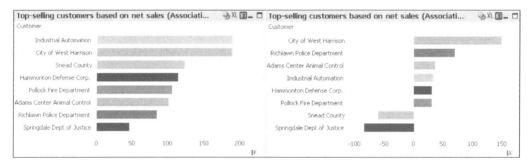

 Examples of the different charts we create in this book are available in accompanying QlikView applications.

Highlighting

The highlighting color technique allows us to quickly detect related or special data within a chart. We use this technique to highlight our products or services when they are benchmarked against those of our competitors, or when we want certain data to stand out to make a point.

We use a light gray to contrast with a dark blue to highlight data. We use a color's shade (that is, lightness or darkness) along with the color's hue (that is, red, green, and blue) to avoid discriminating against those of us who are color blind.

We avoid using red and green hues that are indistinguishable to those of us who are color blind (2 out of 25 men and 1 out of 200 women). We easily involve everybody in our analysis by always contrasting dark colors with the light colors.

Before we apply the highlighting color technique, review steps 1 to 4 of the previous exercise to clone the **Top-selling customers based on net sales** chart, and rename the new chart as `Top-selling customers based on net sales (Highlighting)`.

1. Right-click on the cloned chart object and select **Properties...**
2. In the **General** tab, select the **Show Title in Chart** checkbox and type `Government (blue) vs. other divisions (gray)` in the textbox below the checkbox.
3. Click on **Title Settings...**
4. Click on **Font...** in the **Title Settings** window and select font **Tahoma** and size **8**.
5. In the **Expression** tab, click the plus **(+)** sign next to the **Net Sales expression** to expand its properties.
6. Select **Background Color** and in the **Definition** text area to the right, type the following expression:
   `if(Division='Government',Blue(200),RGB(200,200,200))`
7. Click on **OK**.

Important functions

Let's review some of the functions we used in the previous exercise.

- `Blue(Alpha)`: QlikView has several predefined color functions such as black(), white(), green(), red(), and yellow().The alpha parameter is a number between 0 and 255 and indicates the color's transparency. The alpha value of 0 is completely transparent.

- `RGB(e1,e2,e3)`: A more precise color function defines colors by their red, green, and blue components. Colors used in web pages and for corporate color schemes are usually defined in this manner. Each parameter accepts a number between 0 and 255. A color's RGB code can be found in many websites such as `http://html-colorcodes.com/rgb.html`.

- `If(condition, then, else)`: The If statement in QlikView is similar to the if-statement in Excel. The first parameter contains an expression that is either true or false. If the expression is true, the value of the second parameter is used. Otherwise, if the expression is false, the value of the third parameter is used.

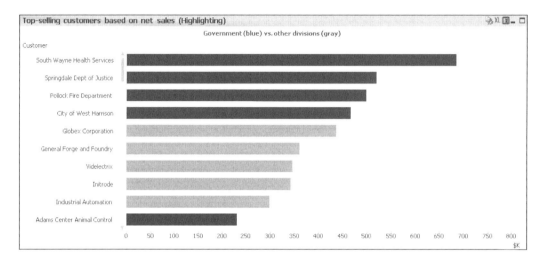

Alerts

We can also compare the bar's value with a reference value, such as budget, forecast, or a value from a previous period of time. We use color to alert the user of something important. For example, the background color of our bar chart could be defined by the following expression:

```
if(sum([Net Sales])<sum([Budgeted Project Revenue])
  ,Red(200),RGB(200,200,200))
```

Heat map

Heat maps use a sequential or diverging color palette to add another metric to the bar chart. Once we review multivariate analysis in *Chapter 4*, *Multivariate Analysis*, and learn how to create heat maps, we can try to include one in a bar chart as shown in the following screenshot:

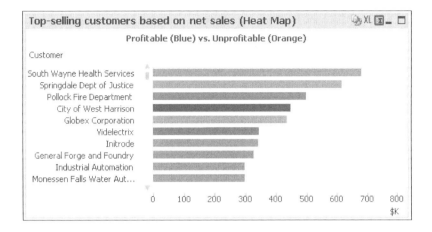

According to the analysis so far, Samantha has concluded that several of the top-selling customers are generating a loss. Let's see how we can increase the data density and understand more about QDataViz, Inc.'s problem.

Rule 3 – add more detail

Along with color we can use other methods to increases a bar chart's data density, or the amount of visible pixels that represent meaningful data within a given space.

Additional dimensions

If we have only one expression defined, we can add up to two additional dimensions to a bar chart. Those dimensions can be grouped, stacked, or made into a trellis chart.

Grouped bar chart

Before we add a second dimension, clone the **Top-selling customers based on net sales** chart and rename the new chart `Top-selling customers based on net sales (Grouped)`.

1. Right-click on the cloned chart object and select **Properties...**

2. In the **Dimensions** tab, select **Product Type** in the **Available Fields/Groups** list and then click on **Add>**.

3. Click on **OK**.

We use grouped bars when there are few values in the dimension that is being grouped, and we want to easily compare each separate element.

Stacked bar chart

An alternative to the grouped chart is a stacked bar chart. Again, let's clone the **Top-selling customers based on net sales** chart and rename the new chart `Top-selling customers based on net sales (Stacked)`.

1. Right-click on the cloned chart object and select **Properties...**
2. In the **Dimensions** tab, select **Product Type** in the **Available Fields/Groups** list and then click on **Add >**.
3. In the **Style** tab, select **Stacked** in the **Subtype** section.
4. Click on **OK**.

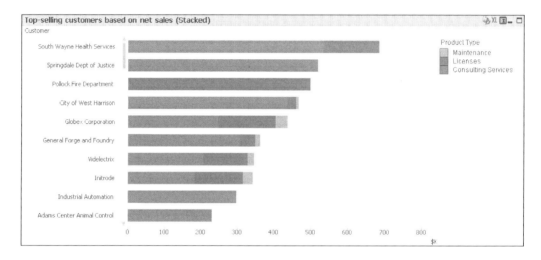

We use stacked bars when we want to compare totals based on one dimension and obtain a general understanding of how the totals are divided among the values of a second dimension. The stacked bar is optimal if it is divided by few values.

Trellis chart

The trellis chart, or small multiples, is a powerful visualization technique that can be applied to any chart. We learn how to create one in *Chapter 3, Trend Analysis*.

Additional expressions

In the same way that additional dimensions are either grouped or stacked, so are additional expressions. We add an additional expression to compare this year's sales value with last year's sales value, one of the most popular analysis techniques.

Set analysis

We implement this technique using a certain syntax called **Set Analysis**. We start with the basics and explore more complex examples in further chapters.

We are currently using the following expression:

```
Sum ([Net Sales])
```

The values calculated from this expression respect the filters we apply in the listboxes. For example, if we select **2013** in the **Year** listbox, the bar chart shows us the top-selling customers of 2013. We use set analysis to automatically apply filters regardless of the ones we manually select.

The first step is to define the underpinning set. The most common base set respects all filters we manually apply in the listboxes, and is represented by {$} as shown in the following expression:

```
Sum ({$} [Net Sales])
```

Conversely, the following base set ignores all filters we manually apply in the listboxes, and is represented by {1} as shown in the following expression:

```
Sum ({1} [Net Sales])
```

The second step is to modify the underpinning set. While respecting all other manual filters, we want one bar to automatically represent the net sales for 2013 without having to select **2013** in the **Year** listbox. We modify the base set with `<Year={2013}>` as shown in the following expression:

```
Sum ({$<Year={2013}>} [Net Sales])
```

Now, let's clone the **Top-selling customers based on net sales** chart, rename the new chart as `Top-selling customers based on net sales (2013 vs. 2012)`, and use the previous expression in our new chart. Perform the following steps:

1. Right-click on the cloned chart object and select **Properties...**

2. In the **Expressions** tab, change the label of **Net Sales** to `2013 Net Sales` and modify its definition to `Sum ({$<Year={2013}>} [Net Sales])`.

3. Right-click on the expression **2013 Net Sales** and select **Copy**.

4. Right-click in the blank space just below the first expression and select **Paste**.

5. Change the label of the new expression to **2012 Net Sales** and the definition to `Sum ({$<Year={2012}>} [Net Sales])`.

6. Click on **OK**.

We can now compare two different years within the same chart as shown in the following screenshot:

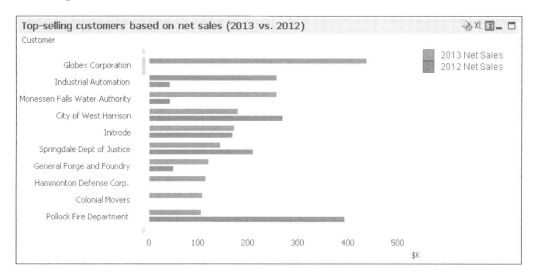

Note that the list of top-selling customers changes in the previous chart because it is sorted by the y-value, or the first metric. Since the first metric is net sales for 2013, the top-selling customers of 2013 appear first.

Although we try to add as much detail as possible, we avoid cramming too much detail into one bar chart. At some point, adding more detail causes more perplexity than clarity. We prefer two separate but intelligible bar charts placed close together instead of one overstuffed bar chart. We look at ways that handle a larger number of variables in *Chapter 4, Multivariate Analysis*.

After adding more detail into our rank analysis, it is now time to take away elements that are not useful.

Rule 4 – throw away chartjunk

Chartjunk is a term coined by *Edward Tufte* in his book, *The Visual Display of Quantitative Information*. He first defined the term data-ink as "ink devoted to the non-redundant display of data-information". Chartjunk is everything else.

We go a step further and consider that we do not deal with static charts in QlikView. Since we perform actions on the charts, we must also consider usability-ink that helps us perform these actions.

In short, we consider chartjunk to be any pixel that is neither data-ink nor usability-ink.

By default, QlikView creates bar charts with little chartjunk. It is therefore our job not to ruin what Qlikview does well.

In our most recent bar chart comparing 2013 net sales with 2012 net sales, the following items appear to be either redundant or non-essential:

- The print icon on the right side of the caption is rarely used
- The word net sales is repeated twice: once in the legend and again in the caption
- The caption background and border around the graph are decorative

The print icon is a waste of space. Lone graphs are rarely printed, and little-used actions do not deserve to occupy space as a shortcut in the caption.

We eliminate the print icon with the following steps:

1. Right-click the chart object and select **Properties...**
2. In the **Caption** tab, clear the **Print** checkbox in the **Special Icons** list.
3. Click on **OK**.

The word net sales is redundant data-ink; however, it is not redundant usability-ink. If we eliminate the word net sales from the metric labels and then export the chart to Excel, we will lose all mention of net sales in Excel.

Finally, the caption background and border is not data-ink, but it is usability-ink since we use these elements to easily move and resize the chart. The default pale gray used for these elements is perfect. We resist making these elements follow a corporate color scheme since most corporate color schemes contain dark, vivid colors that distract from our data analysis.

Rule 5 – respect usability

After reviewing several rules that augment a chart's capacity to visualize data, we now focus on how to optimize a chart's usability. We center our attention on two areas: the caption and inside the chart.

Caption

The default caption shortcuts include **Export to Excel**, **Minimize**, and **Maximize**. Two other useful shortcuts are Copy Image to Clipboard and Fast Change.

Export to Excel

Some elements in a chart may not export to Excel as we would hope, so we always verify the results exporting a chart to Excel.

Minimize

We verify that when we minimize a chart, the icon is visible and readily available to restore the chart.

Maximize

We verify that when we maximize a chart, the resulting chart is legible. If a chart has a transparent background, it can be hard to understand when we maximize it over other charts.

Copy Image to Clipboard

When we export a bar chart to Excel, we may expect to see that same bar chart in Excel rather than the tabular data that is actually exported. For this reason, we add the **Copy Image to Clipboard** shortcut.

1. Right-click on a chart object and select **Properties...**
2. In the **Caption** tab, select the **Copy Image to Clipboard** checkbox in the **Special Icons** list.
3. Click on **OK**.

Fast change

Also, we would like to change graphs into tables or other types of graphs. Therefore, we add a shortcut to readily change the type of chart we are viewing.

1. Right-click on a chart object and select **Properties...**
2. In the **General** tab, select the **Bar Chart** checkbox and the **Straight Table** checkbox in the **Fast Type Change** list on the lower right-hand side of the window.
3. Click on **OK**.

Inside the chart

By default, QlikView creates a small, subdued scrollbar that is hard to use. The scrollbar should not compete with the data so it should remain subdued; however, we prefer to make it wider so that we can more easily scroll though the chart. Perform the following steps:

1. Right-click on a chart object and select **Properties...**

2. In the **Layout** tab, type 14 in the **Scrollbar Width** textbox in the **Scrollbars** section.

3. Click on **OK**.

Now that we've talked about the chart's display and usability, the next step is to talk about how we want it to be interpreted.

Rule 6 – be honest

As the 19th century phrase goes:

> *"There are three kinds of lies: lies, damned lies, and statistics."*

Sadly, data visualization, like statistics, is used to support fallacious arguments.

Chart width to height ratio

All charts can suffer from width and height manipulation that exaggerates or hides variations. We may temporarily change a chart's size while looking for patterns or anomalies in the data, but we set limits that discourage distorting the data. We recommend a chart's aspect ratio to be between 1:1 and 2:1.

Although we can change the chart object's width and height in the **Caption** tab of its **Chart Properties** window. The width and height of the chart itself can be manipulated in the following manner:

1. Select a chart object and press *Crtl+Shift*.

2. Resize the bar chart outlined in red within the chart object. We may need to first move or reduce the size of other components (for example, legend) in order to enlarge the chart.

3. If necessary, in the **General** tab, click on **Reset User Sizing** and **Reset User Docking** to restore the components' original size and location.

Axis not forced to zero

The next bar chart manipulation we avoid is clearing the **Force 0** checkbox in the **Axes** tab. Even if the bars in a chart represent huge numbers, and in effect, show little difference between them, we risk exaggerating differences if we let QlikView choose some arbitrary starting point that is not 0. It may even appear that the value of one bar is 100 percent greater than that of another, even though the real difference is less than 1 percent. In conclusion, keep the **Forced 0** checkbox selected for bar charts.

Before moving on to trend analysis, we save our QlikView application.

1. Click on Save ⊞ in the standard toolbar.

Summary

We use rank analysis to focus on important aspects of our company. We execute rank analysis using bar charts and we make effective bar charts using the data visualization style guide. The style guide consists of the following rules:

*   Rule 1 – use adequate labeling
*   Rule 2 – convert color into data
*   Rule 3 – add more detail
*   Rule 4 – throw away chartjunk
*   Rule 5 – respect usability
*   Rule 6 – be honest

Samantha has discovered the top-selling customers of QDataViz, Inc. She has also discovered how each customer's sales are divided between our product types and whether the customer has meant a profit or a loss to the company. If we focus on these top-selling customers, we have a good chance of solving our company's problems. Let's continue our analysis of QDataViz, Inc. and see how it has performed over time.

3

Trend Analysis

Whether we are analyzing data from a human resources department, a finance department, a government agency, or a nonprofit organization, we can be sure that a part of that analysis will consider a time-related dimension. Analyzing the change over time is called **trend analysis**.

What is trend analysis?

More than just analyzing the values associated with certain time periods, trend analysis is the analysis of the rate of growth or decline between different periods of time. We can choose to compare any hour, day, month, or year with any other hour, day, month, or year. Also, we can visualize a trend in both real values and percentage changes.

Samantha's next task is to analyze if QDataViz, Inc.'s losses have grown over time. First, Samantha may analyze the company's month after month sales growth. However, she may also evaluate seasonal trends by visualizing the percentage changes between the same months of different years or the percentage change between each month of 2013 and a base month, such as January 2013. Again, she has a wide variety of methods to perform a trend analysis.

We recommend using a line chart or a bar chart for trend analysis. The line chart focuses our attention on the rate of change between time periods, while the bar chart focuses our attention on comparing the discrete values of each time period.

Since we reviewed the bar chart in the previous chapter, let's now review the line chart.

The line chart

Let's create a new sheet and then a line chart to analyze QDataViz, Inc.'s month after month sales growth using the following steps:

1. Open the QlikView application `Sales_Project_Analysis_Sandbox.qvw`.

2. Create a new sheet and call it `Trend Analysis`.

3. Click on **Create Chart** [icon] in the design toolbar.

4. Again, let's consider the three steps necessary to create any chart as shown in the following diagram:

   1. Choose the desired type of chart. Select the line chart (pictured earlier) and click on **Next >**.

   2. Choose a dimension that groups the metric defined in the next step. Since we want to see month after month sales growth, the dimension is month/year. So, in the **Available Fields/Groups** list on the left side of the window double-click on **Month/Year**. Click **Next >**.

   3. Define a metric, or an expression. Since we want to see month after month sales growth, the metric is the sum of the sales. So, in the **Edit Expression** window, type `Sum ([Net Sales])`. Click on **OK**, and then click on **Finish**.

Although the resulting chart, as shown in the following screenshot, is poorly formatted, we now have a basic line chart:

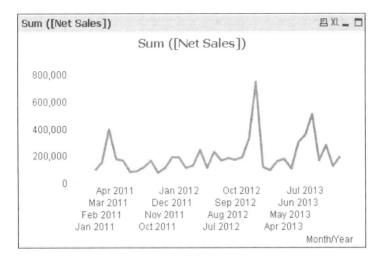

Objects to support line charts

As we did in the previous chapter, we add listboxes for month, year, division, and product type to the **Trend Analysis** sheet. We also add the search object and current selections object to occasionally filter the line chart and enrich our analysis.

Data visualization style guide for line charts

The data visualization style guides for line charts and bar charts are quite similar. Let's reinforce some principles and add a few new ones that are particular to line charts.

Rule 1 – use adequate labeling

All components of a chart should be made coherent by adequate labeling. We will use **Tahoma** as the font for all the labels and use a font size between 8 and 10.

Chart labels

The first label should convey the intention of the chart to the audience. Repeat the same steps we performed for the bar chart to make the following changes:

1. Change the caption title to `Net sales by month/year` in the **General** tab.

2. Change the font to **Tahoma** and the font size to **10** in the **Caption** tab.

3. Remove the title located within the chart in the **General** tab.

Dimension and metric labels

There is no explicit label that describes the line in the graph, as it is obvious from the title that we are looking at net sales. However, the dimension and metric labels appear in a pop-up window, and later on they will appear in a legend as we add additional dimensions and metrics to the chart.

Again, in the same way as we defined the dimension and expression labels for the bar chart, define the dimension label to be **Month/Year** and the expression label to be **Net Sales**.

We consider three differences between the labeling of bar charts and line charts.

- Time-series line charts are traditionally viewed left to right, so we never change the orientation of a line chart to a vertical orientation.

- In the **Expressions** tab, as in the bar chart, we have the option to show the numeric values of the metric in the chart by selecting the **Values on Data Points** checkbox. However, the numeric values in the line charts may overlap; so we sometimes select the **Vertical** checkbox in the **Values on Data Points** section within the **Presentation** tab to prevent overlapping.

- Also in the **Expressions** tab, we select the **Symbol** checkbox in the **Display Options** section if we want the value of each month to stand out. We select an appropriate symbol in the adjacent drop-down list, and if necessary we change the **Symbol Size** in the **Presentation** tab.

Axes labels

The final labels to consider are the axes labels. Step 2 and step 3 are similar to the actions we performed on the bar chart.

1. Right-click on the chart object and select **Properties…**.

2. In the **Number** tab, define **Net Sales** as an integer and assign **$, $K,** and **$M** to the **Symbol, Thousand Symbol,** and **Million Symbol** textboxes, respectively.

3. In the **Axes** tab, change the **Expression Axes** and the **Dimension Axis** font to **Tahoma** and the font size to **8**.

4. In the **Axes** tab, select the **/** option for the **Primary Dimension** label.

5. In the **Presentation** tab, select the **Enable X-Axis Scrollbar** checkbox, type 13 in the **When Number of Items Exceeds:** textbox, and select the **Reversed** checkbox.

We choose to view 13 months so that we can see a whole year and compare the most recent month with the same month last year. Selecting the **Reversed** checkbox automatically moves the scrollbar so as to show the most recent months.

The following chart is the result of the previous exercises:

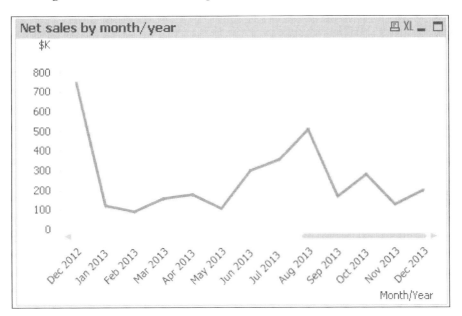

Rule 2 – convert color into data

We use color in line charts so that users can easily identify each line. We propose three coloring techniques for line charts: associative, highlighting, and referential.

Associative

We perform the same steps that we learned in the previous chapter to implement the associative coloring technique.

Dynamic highlighting

We've already seen how to apply the highlighting color technique for bar charts. Since it's the same procedure for line charts, let's take advantage of the line chart to show how to include dynamic highlighting in QlikView.

Before starting the following steps, clone the **Net sales by month/year** chart and rename the new chart Net sales by month/year and product type (Dynamic Highlighting).

1. Right-click on the cloned chart and select **Properties...**.
2. In the **Dimensions** tab, double-click on **Product Type** in the **Available Fields/Groups** list.

Set analysis

In listboxes, values excluded from our filters remain visible and are gray-colored; however QlikView hides excluded data in charts. We use set analysis to change this default behavior.

We remember from the previous chapter that Sum ({$} [Net Sales]) defines a base set that respects the filters we apply in the listboxes. We deduce that Sum ({$<[Product Type]={'Licenses'}>} [Net Sales]) calculates the net sales for licenses on top of the base set.

If we don't assign a value to a field in set analysis, the expression will ignore any filter that is directly applied to that field. Even if we select **Licenses** in the **Product Type** listbox, the following expression still calculates net sales for every product type:

```
Sum ({$<[Product Type]= >} [Net Sales])
```

Let's go back to the application of dynamic highlighting to our line chart:

1. In the **Expression** tab, replace the current expression in **Net Sales** with
   Sum({$<[Product Type]= >} [Net Sales]).
2. Click on the plus sign (+) next to **Net Sales** to expand its properties.
3. Select **Background Color** and type the following expression in the **Definition** textbox to the right:
   ```
   if(not match(only({1} [Product Type]),
   $(=concat(distinct chr(39) & [Product Type] &
   ```

```
    chr(39),',')))), argb(200,200,200,200)
)
```

Now, if we select certain product types, we notice that those items are highlighted, while the other product types are still visible, but colored in gray. This coloring technique is great for focusing on the behavior of a few variables without losing sight of the whole picture.

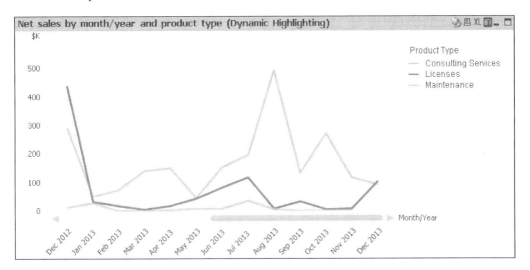

Important functions

In short, the background color expression mentioned earlier evaluates whether a product type is in the list of selected product types and, if it is not selected, its corresponding line is colored in gray. Within this loaded expression, we notice several useful functions.

- `match( str, expr1 [ , expr2,...exprN ] )`: If we want to compare an expression or field with a series of values, we use the match function. Instead of typing `if(field=1 or field=2 or field=3`, we type `match(field,1,2,3,…)`. The match function has several variations. The most common variation is `wildmatch()` that accepts a list of values with wildcards. The `not` keyword before the `match()` function returns TRUE when the field doesn't match a value in the list.

- `only( expression )`: Instead of aggregating values as the `sum()` or `avg()` functions do, the `only()` function returns a value only when one unique value exists. Otherwise, it returns `null`. The set analysis `{1}` is necessary to ignore any filter manually applied.

- `$(=expression )`: Dollar-sign expansion is a technique to precalculate an embedded expression before calculating the final expression. For example, we use the `match()` function because we want to see if a product type is currently selected. However, the list of values that are currently selected is dynamic, so we dynamically define the list of values in the `match()` function. If **Licenses** is selected, the dollar sign expansion returns the following `match()` function:

  ```
  match(only({1} [Product Type]),'Licenses')
  ```

  If **Licenses** and **Consulting Services** are selected, we obtain the following the `match()` function:

  ```
  match(only({1} [Product Type]),'Licenses','Consulting Services')
  ```

- `concat ([ distinct ] expression [,` We usually aggregate numeric values, but text, or string, values can also be aggregated. The `concat()` function returns a list of texts from multiple rows of data. If the `distinct` keyword is used, then only a list of unique texts is returned.

- `chr( n )`: Text values in QlikView are always encased within single quotes. When we want to add single quotes to the result of our dollar-sign expansion, we use the `chr()` function. The number we use in the `chr()` function corresponds to the ASCII code of the character we want. The character code for a single quote is 39. The ampersand (&) concatenates text.

- `ARGB(alpha, e1, e2, e3)`: It is similar to the `RGB()` function we reviewed in the previous chapter. The `ARGB()` function adds an alpha parameter that determines a color's transparency. The alpha value of 0 is completely transparent while the alpha value of 255 is completely opaque.

References

The last coloring technique helps us to identify references without having to lose time in moving our eyes back and forth from the legend to the line chart.

Before starting the following steps, clone the **Net sales by month/year** chart and rename the new chart as `Net sales year-over-year vs. budget (References)`:

1. Right-click on the cloned chart and select **Properties...**.

2. In the **Dimensions** tab, remove the field **Month/Year** from the **Used Dimensions** list, and add **Month**.

3. In the **Expressions** tab, change the label of **Net Sales** to **2013 Net Sales** and modify its definition to `Sum ({$<Year={2013}>} [Net Sales])`.

4. Right-click on the expression **2013 Net Sales** and click on **Copy**.

5. Right-click in the blank space just below the first expression and click on **Paste**.

6. Change the label of the new expression to **2012 Net Sales** and the definition to Sum ({$<Year={2012}>} [Net Sales]).

7. Again, right-click in the blank space just below the second expression and click on **Paste**.

8. Change the label of the new expression to **2013 Sales Budget** and the definition to Sum ({$<Year={2013}>} [Sales Budget]).

9. In the **Expression** tab, click on the plus (+) sign next to the **2013 Sales Budget** expression to expand its properties.

10. Select **Line Style** and in the **Definition** textarea to the right, type '<s2>'. There are a total of four available line styles. '<s1>' is the normal style and '<s2>', '<s3>', and '<s4>' are the different dotted line styles.

We use a dotted line for budgets and forecasts to denote something that is not yet real.

11. In the **Colors** tab, we define the first color button to be dark blue, the second color button to be light blue, and the third color button to be light gray.

We can copy and paste colors if we right-click on a colored button that has the color we want and select **Copy**. Then right-click on the destination color button and select **Paste All**.

12. Optionally, click on the second and third color button and define the transparency to be around **25%** in the **Transparency** slider.

13. Click on **OK**.

The choice of colors is based on the idea that lighter colors of the same hue can be interpreted as being faded by age. Therefore last year is a lighter shade of blue. The budget is gray so that the line representing **2013 Net Sales** stands out against two pale reference lines.

The result of the previous exercise is shown in the following screenshot:

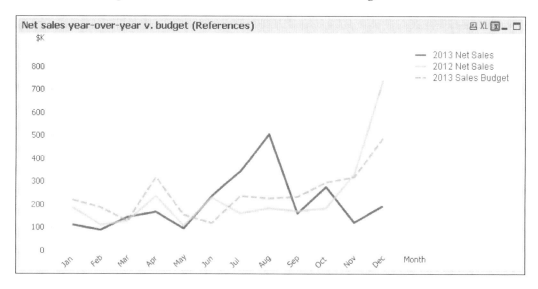

Rule 3 – add more detail

We've already added more detail and increased the data density while reviewing the previous rule, but let's see how much more data we can add.

Additional dimension

Even when we are displaying more than one metric, we can add an additional dimension and convert the line chart into a trellis chart.

Trellis chart

Before starting the following steps, clone the **Net sales year-over-year vs. budget (References)** chart and rename the new chart as Net sales year-over-year vs. budget (Trellis).

1. Right-click on the cloned chart and select **Properties...**.
2. In the **Dimensions** tab, double-click on **Division** in the **Available Fields/ Groups** list.
3. Select **Division** in the **Used Dimensions** list and click on **Promote**.
4. In the same tab, click on **Trellis...**.
5. In the **Trellis Settings** window, select the **Enable Trellis Chart** checkbox.

6. Select the **Fixed** option in both **Number of Columns** and **Number of Rows**.

7. Type 2 in the textboxes to the right of the **Fixed** option in both sections.

The scale of the axes of all the line charts is the same, so we can easily compare the trend between the different line charts.

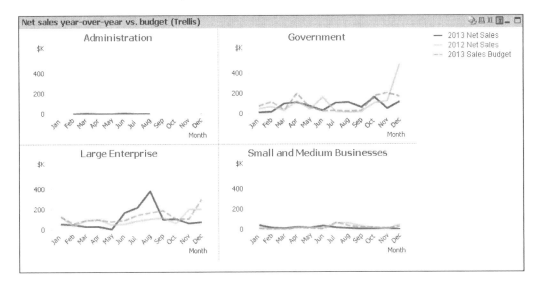

Additional metric

We've already created a line chart with various metrics, but those metrics were measured against the same axis scale. We can also add an additional metric that uses a different axis scale.

Before starting the following steps, clone the **Net sales by month/year** chart and rename the new chart as Net sales and % profit margin by month/year:

1. Right-click on the cloned chart object and select **Properties...**.

2. In the **Expressions** tab, click on **Add**, type Sum ([Profit Margin])/Sum ([Net Sales]) in the **Edit Expression** window, and then click on **OK**. Change the label of the new metric to % Profit Margin.

3. In the **Numbers** tab, select **% Profit Margin** from the list of expressions on the left, select the **Integer** option, and the **Show in Percent(%)** checkbox. Type % in **Symbol** textbox.

4. In the **Axes** tab, select **% Profit Margin** from the list of expressions in the upper, left-hand corner and select the **Right (Top)** option. Optionally, we can select the **Split Axis** checkbox, and create two separate charts within the same object.

5. Click on **OK** as shown in the following screenshot:

We can now analyze the relationship between the tendency of net sales and of the profit margin percentage within the same graph.

Rule 4 – throw away chartjunk

Almost all the ink in the line charts are used for data or usability. Similar to bar charts, we recommend removing the print icon from the caption.

Axis and grid lines

By default, QlikView does not draw axis or grid lines. In most cases, these elements are **chartjunk**. Instead of a grid based on arbitrary numbers, we do sometimes find it important to include an important threshold. If, for example, a metric floats between positive and negative numbers, and it is vital that we identify quickly if the number is positive or negative at each point in the line chart, we can add a reference line at zero in the **Presentation** tab and symbols to the line in the **Expression** tab.

Otherwise, if there is some analytical benefit for adding a generic grid, we can do so in the **Axes** tab of the chart properties window. Both the **Expression Axes** and the **Dimension Axis** section have a **Show Grid** checkbox. When we add a grid, it never interferes with the real data. Therefore, we define the grid to be pale gray, dashed line.

Rule 5 – respect usability

The line chart has the same usability features as the bar chart.

Caption

The caption should include the following icons:

- Export to Excel
- Minimize
- Maximize
- Copy image to Clipboard
- Fast change

The fast change options should include the straight table, the bar chart, and the radar chart.

The radar charts are nothing more than a fancy way to draw a line chart and should not be used as a default view; but rather, the radar chart can be used as a fast change option that the user selects.

Inside the chart

Similar to the bar chart in the previous chapter, the scroll bar in our line chart should be 14 points wide. We can also increase the usability of the chart if we add a dimensional group.

Dimensional group

A dimensional group can be a cyclic group or a drill-down group. These groups allow us to change the chart's dimension or drilldown into another dimension with just one click.

The drill-down group is usually a series of dimensions that define a strict hierarchy. For example, **Year**, **Quarter**, **Month**, and **Day** compose a suitable hierarchy. Cyclical groups are usually groups of related and unrelated dimensions such as, **Customer**, **Division**, **Product Type**, and **Account Manager**.

Before starting the following steps, clone the **Net sales by month/year** chart and rename the new chart as Net sales by month/year (Dimensional Group):

1. Right-click on the cloned chart object and select **Properties...**.
2. In the **Dimensions** tab, click on **Edit Group...**.
3. Under the **Groups** list, click on **New...**.

4. Type `clDivision_ProductType` in the **Group Name** textbox, and select the **Cyclic Group** option.

5. In the **Available Fields** list on the left-hand side of the window, double-click on the fields **Product Type** and **Division**.

6. In the **Dimensions** tab, select the group **clDivision_ProductType** from the **Available Fields/Groups** list on the left-hand side of the window, and click on **Add >**.

We are now able to click on the circular yellow arrow and toggle between viewing the line chart by division and product type. We display the whole list of available dimensions by clicking on the small, black arrow on the right-hand side of the circular yellow arrow.

We do the same procedure to create a drill-down group. We can also reuse the groups among multiple charts.

Rule 6 – being honest

Be careful not to purposely manipulate a line chart so as to show more or less growth.

Chart width to height ratio

The same rule applies to line charts as it does to bar charts. The line chart is more susceptible to width manipulation because the degree of inclination or declination of a line is interpreted as a value's rate of growth or contraction. For example, a tall and narrow line chart can be used to falsely show dramatic growth. The following screenshots are the same line chart with different width to height ratios:

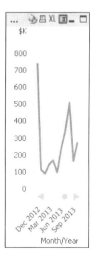

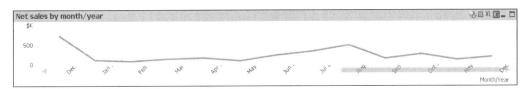

Axis not forced to zero

Unlike bar charts that compare discrete values, line charts focus our attention on rates of change. Therefore, we do not have to force the axis to zero. We can clear the **Forced 0** checkbox in the **Presentation** tab of the chart's properties.

Before moving on to multivariate analysis, we should save our QlikView application. So, click on **Save** in the standard toolbar.

Summary

Trend analysis is a universal analysis technique suitable for all data sources. Trend analysis is best done with line charts, and occasionally, with bar charts. The data visualization style guide for line charts is similar to that of the bar chart.

Samantha has now realized that QDataViz, Inc.'s losses have been prevalent throughout the last three years. Since its losses are not dependent on time, what other variable could be causing the losses? We've been able to add more variables to our bar charts and line charts, but each has its limits as to how many variables can be added. Let's see how multivariate analysis helps us to add even more variables to our charts.

4
Multivariate Analysis

In the previous two chapters we have shown Samantha how to take advantage of limited space and insert as much detail and information as possible within bar charts and line charts. However, many of her previous spreadsheets were tables packed with several dimensions and metrics. Until now, we've only been able to manage charts with one or two dimensions and one or two metrics. Placing charts side-by-side is one solution, but let's look at a couple of other options available.

What is multivariate analysis?

What makes multivariate analysis different from the previous types of analysis is the number of variables that we want to compare in the same chart. Although comparing one metric between the values of one or two dimensions (for example, net sales by division and product type) has been insightful, Samantha is looking for various ways to help her analyze a few large spreadsheet reports. For example, one report compares four metrics: net sales, profit margin, number of consultants, and consultant days worked.

Multivariate analysis involves looking for patterns. For example, we might discover a group of customers that have high net sales, a low profit margin, numerous consultants, and a large amount of consultant days worked.

No chart is perfect for multivariate analysis, so we will use various chart types that help our eyes detect patterns. First, we are going to use a table chart to create a heat map, and then we are going to embed mini-charts into both a straight table chart and a pivot table chart.

Table charts

Table charts are probably the most popular charts created to analyze and look up data. They can either present a detailed view of data represented graphically or contain data that cannot be easily made into any other chart. While large table charts are great for looking up detailed data, they are not optimal for analysis because our minds struggle to find patterns within tables filled with numbers. For example, the following table doesn't tell us very efficiently if there is a relationship between net sales, profit margin, days worked, and number of consultants.

Customer KPI's (Normal Table)				XL _ □
Customer /	Net Sales	Profit Margin	Days Worked	Num. of Consultants
	7,117,977	**1,064,307**	**63,835**	**438**
South Wayne Health Services	680,056	-38,558	3,985	57
Springdale Dept of Justice	519,388	-94,707	5,546	25
Pollock Fire Department	498,542	109,748	0	0
City of West Harrison	447,895	323,035	2,594	22
Globex Corporation	436,584	-4,648	2,404	36
Videlectrix	345,887	173,188	1,598	22
Initrode	342,415	55,055	3,434	29
General Forge and Foundry	328,959	75,888	4,447	38

We help our pattern-seeking minds to analyze tables by adding visual cues to them.

Heat map

Let's create a heat map in a new sheet that is a copy of the **Trend Analysis** sheet. In this way, we can save time and reuse the same listboxes, search object, and current selections object.

1. Open the QlikView document `Sales_Project_Analysis_Sandbox.qvw`.

2. Right-click over an empty space in the **Trend Analysis** sheet. Select **Copy Sheet**.

3. In the **Copy of Trend Analysis** sheet, delete all the line chart objects and rename the sheet as `Multivariate Analysis`.

4. After performing the exercises of the previous two chapters, we should now know the basics of creating charts and navigating the chart properties window. From this point on, let's avoid including the detailed instructions of what we've already done.

Let's create a chart with the following characteristics.

Type of chart	Straight table (as shown in preceding diagram)
Dimension	Customer
First metric	sum([Net Sales])
Second metric	sum([Profit Margin])
Third metric	sum([Days Worked])
Fourth metric	count(distinct Employee)

We now have a basic straight table that looks similar to an unformatted version of the Customer KPI's table shown earlier. Let's go to the **Chart Properties** window and follow the given steps for each expression to make this table chart into a heat map:

1. In the **Expressions** tab, click on the plus (+) sign next to the expression to expand its properties.

2. Select **Background Color** and click on **...** in the **Definition** textbox to the right.

3. In the **File** menu of the **Edit Expression** window, select **Colormix Wizard...**.

4. Click on **Next >**.

5. Type the same expression used to define the metric in the **Value Expression** textbox. For example, if we are defining the background color for sum([Net Sales]), then type sum([Net Sales]) in the **Value Expression** textbox. Click on **Next >**.

> If we create a heat map in a bar chart, we define the heat map using a different expression than the one defined as the metric. For example, the heat map within the bar chart shown in *Chapter 2, Rank Analysis*, defines the heat map using profit margin even though the metric is net sales.

6. Click on the green color button below the **Upper Limit** textbox.

7. In the **Color Area** window, again click on the green color button.

8. In the **Color** window, select blue.

9. Click on **OK** twice.

10. Click on the red button below the **Lower Limit** textbox and follow steps similar to steps 7 through 9 to select an orange color.

 When we want the heat map to distinguish between positive and negative values, we select the Intermediate checkbox and type 0 in the Intermediate text box. We recommend using a light gray as the Intermediate color.

11. Click on **Next >**.

12. Click on **Finish**.

13. Click on **OK**.

14. Repeat steps 2 through 13 for each expression.

15. In the **Sort** tab, select **Customer** in the **Priority** list, and promote it to the top of the list. Select the **Expression** checkbox and select **Descending** in the drop-down box to the right. Type sum([Net Sales]) in the textbox below the **Expression** checkbox.

16. Click on **OK**.

We now have the following heat map:

sum([Net Sales])				🖳 XL _ ☐
Customer	sum([Net Sal...	sum([Profit ...	sum([Days W...	count(distinct...
	#####	#####	63835	438
South Wayne Health Services	660055.32562868	-38557.740787445	3985	57
Springdale Dept of Justice	519307.57550176	-94706.910660622	5546	25
Pollock Fire Department	498542.07147984	109748.26024623	0	0
City of West Harrison	447894.5274817	323035.16305933	2594	22
Globex Corporation	436583.93631649	-4648.4831737306	2404	36
Videlectrix	345886.89959275	173180.34627168	1598	22
Initrode	342415.46554766	55055.197843555	3434	29
General Forge and Foundry	328958.96479165	75887.721673673	4447	38
Industrial Automation	299384.80346616	-49854.554219922	5257	33
Monessen Falls Water Authority	299384.80346616	-49854.554219922	5257	33
Input, Inc.	204231.94833948	-13636.391513007	3064	46
West Pepperell Municipal Serv...	181471.27396274	181471.27396274	0	0
Charles Townsend Agency	181129.90704595	-116103.58105504	1747	6

Various adjustments are necessary to make it more readable, but before reviewing the data visualization style guide for table charts, let's create another table chart with embedded mini-charts.

Mini-charts

First, let's add mini-charts to a straight table and then to a pivot table.

Straight table for multiple metrics

A straight table is excellent when we have one dimension and multiple metrics.

Let's create the same chart as the previous one with the following characteristics:

Type of chart	Straight table (as shown in preceding diagram)
Dimension	Customer
First metric	sum([Net Sales])
Second metric	sum([Profit Margin])
Third metric	sum([Days Worked])
Fourth metric	count(distinct Employee)

Instead of converting the table chart into a heat map, let's add mini-charts to it. Let's go to the **Chart Properties** window and follow the given steps:

1. In the **Expressions** tab, copy and paste each metric twice.
2. Use **Promote** and **Demote** to sort the metrics so that those with the same expression are positioned next to each other. In the end, there should be three consecutive instances of the same metric.
3. In the second instance of each metric, select the **Mini Chart** option in the **Representation** drop-down box.
4. Click on **Mini Chart Settings**.
5. In the **Dimension** drop-down box select **Month/Year**.
6. Click on **OK**.
7. In the third instance of each metric, select the **Linear Gauge** option in the **Representation** drop-down box.
8. Click on **Gauge Settings**.

9. In the **Gauge Properties** window, type one of the corresponding expressions into the **Max** textbox.

    ° For the metric sum([Net Sales]), type max(aggr(sum([Net Sales]),Customer))

    ° For the metric sum([Profit Margin]), type max(aggr(sum([Profit Margin]),Customer))

    ° For the metric sum([Days Worked]), type max(aggr(sum([Days Worked]),Customer))

    ° For the metric count(distinct Employee), type max(aggr(count(distinct Employee),Customer))

10. Clear the **Autowidth Segments** checkbox.

11. Select the **Hide Gauge Outlines** checkbox.

12. Clear the **Show Scale** checkbox.

13. Select the **Fill to Value** option in the **Mode** drop-down box.

14. Select **Segment1** in the **Segments Setup** section, and change **Color** to blue.

15. Select **Segment2** and click on **Delete**.

16. Click on **OK**.

17. Once all the expressions have a mini-chart and a linear gauge, click on **OK**.

We should now have something similar to the following table chart that we will improve on later with the data visualization style guide for table charts:

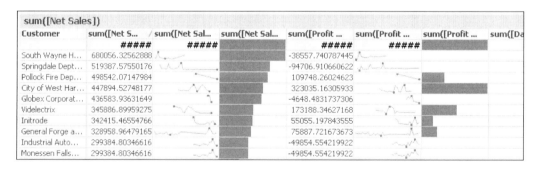

Important functions

Let's take a closer look at the new function we used recently:

- `aggr ([ distinct | nodistinct ] [{set_expression}]expression {, dimension})`: The advanced aggregation function returns a list of values that are the result of the given expression segmented by the given dimension. The expression `aggr(sum([Net Sales]),Customer)` creates a list of numeric values that are the sum of net sales grouped by the customer. Therefore, `max(aggr(sum([Net Sales]),Customer))` returns the maximum amount of net sales of any customer. This result is different from what `max([Net Sales])` returns, which is the maximum amount of net sales of any transaction.

Pivot table for multiple dimensions

A pivot table is excellent when we have multiple dimensions and few metrics.

Let's create a pivot table chart with the following characteristics:

Type of chart	Pivot Table (as shown in preceding diagram)
Dimensions	Division, Customer, and Year
Metric	sum([Net Sales])

The result of the previous exercise is a basic pivot table that has all of its dimensions collapsed. Now, let's adjust the pivot table's dimensions and add a mini-chart to it.

1. Right-click over the column **Division** and select **Expand All**. Do the same for the column **Customer**.

2. Click-and-drag the column **Year** to the area above the column sum([Net Sales]). It sometimes takes a little patience, but once a blue arrow pointing left appears above the column sum([Net Sales]), release the mouse button.

Net Sales by Division / Customer and Year (USD $)			
Division	Customer	Year	Net Sales
	⊟ **Total**		**3,177,468**
	Globex Corporation ⊟	2013	436,584
	⊟	2011	160,491

3. Right-click on the table chart object and select **Properties...**.

4. In the **Expressions** tab, copy and paste the sum([Net Sales]) metric.

5. In the new sum([Net Sales]) metric, select the **Linear Gauge** option in the **Representation** drop-down box.

6. Click on **Gauge Settings**.

7. In the **Gauge Properties** window, type max(aggr(sum([Net Sales]),Division,Year)) in the **Max** textbox.

8. Clear the **Autowidth Segments** checkbox.

9. Select the **Hide Gauge Outlines** checkbox.

10. Clear the **Show Scale** checkbox.

11. Select the **Fill to Value** option in the **Mode** drop-down box.

12. Select **Segment1** in the **Segments Setup** section, and change **Color** to blue.

13. Select **Segment2** and click on **Delete**.

14. Click on **OK**.

15. In the **Sort** tab, select **Division** in the **Priority** list. Select the **Expression** checkbox and select **Descending** in the drop-down list to the right. Type sum([Net Sales]) in the textbox below the **Expression** checkbox.

16. Repeat step 15 for **Customer**.

17. Click on **OK**.

We now have the following pivot table, which we will make ready for effective analysis and communication in the next section.

sum([Net Sales])						🖳 XL _ ☐
	Year		2011		2012		2013
Division	Customer	sum([Net Sales])	sum([Net Sales])	sum([Net Sales])	sum([Net Sales])	sum([Net Sales])	sum([Net Sales])
Large Enterprise ⊞		633767.95382729		1242521.1131896		1301178.6470367	
	⊟ South Wayne H…	529969.82576388		150086.499865		-	
	Springdale Dept…	263296.95568468		209780.4198947		46310.199922374	
	Pollock Fire Dep…	-		392964.65039713		105577.42108271	
	City of West Har…	-		267964.5197912		179930.00769058	
	Industrial Auto…	-		-		189333.09333093	
	Monessen Falls…	-		-		189333.09333093	
	West Pepperell…	-		80492.799927999		100978.47403474	
	Hammonton De…	-		-		114048.89258393	
	Snead County	-		59792.289172892		52759.715174152	
	Burton Police	108634.14274255		-		-	
Government	City of Bunnell	38606.193849563		42416.861134527		-	

Data visualization style guide for table charts

Although table charts are not graphs, it is just as important to respect a few rules so that they can be more easily understood.

Rule 1 – use adequate labeling

All components of a chart should be made coherent by adequate labeling.
We will use Tahoma as the font of all labels and use a font size between 8 and 10.

Chart labels

In the **Window Title** textbox within the **General** tab of the **Chart Properties** window, include a chart label that explains the purpose of the table chart and describes the characteristics common to all the columns (for example, USD $, EUR €, Kg, L, Ton, and so on). For example, Customer KPI Heat Map (blue = high, orange = low), Customer KPI Comparison or Net Sales by Division / Customer and Year (USD $).

Dimension and metric labels

First, if necessary, we modify the dimension label in the **Label** textbox within the **Dimensions** tab of the **Chart Properties** window.

Second, in the **Label** textbox within the **Expressions** tab, include a metric label that explains what the numeric value or mini-chart describes. Since table charts don't have axes, include the unit of measure in the expression label if it has not already been included in the chart label.

If set analysis is used to automatically filter the metric, then include the automatic filters in the label. For example, the label of a metric that always calculates the previous year should be **Net Sales (Last Year)**, **Net Sales (LY)**, or **Net Sales (2012)**.

Column labels should be horizontally aligned in the same fashion as the values within the column. Also, we prevent a column label from being only partially visible by making the column header row two lines tall.

Let's do the following steps in the **Chart Properties** window to increase the label row's height, and horizontally align all the labels that describe columns containing numbers to the right:

1. In the **Presentation** tab, select the columns that contain numbers in the **Columns** list in the upper left-hand corner, and select the **Right** option to the right-hand side of **Label** in the **Alignment** section.

2. In the same tab, select the **Wrap Header Text** checkbox. Note that the **Header Height** is **2** lines.

3. Click on **OK**.

We add **Month/Year** to the column labels above the mini line charts and **Ranking** to the column labels above the embedded bar charts. For example, the complete labels for the net sales mini line charts would be **Net Sales Month/Year** and **Net Sales Ranking** for the embedded bar charts. **Column totals** and **subtotals** are automatically shown in straight tables but, in some cases, these totals are not necessary. In the **Chart Properties** window, let's remove the totals above the mini-charts.

1. In the **Expressions** tab, for each column that contains a mini-chart or a linear gauge, select **No Totals** in the **Total Mode** section.

2. Click on **OK**.

Customer KPI Comparison						
Customer	Net Sales (USD $)	Net Sales Month/Year	Net Sales Ranking	Profit Margin (USD $)	Profit Margin Month/Year	Profit Margin Ranking
	7,117,977			1,083,211		

Conversely, in pivot tables, we have to manually enable subtotals. In the **Chart Properties** window, we enable subtotals so that we can see a dimension value's total even if the value is expanded.

1. In the **Presentation** tab, select **Customer** in the list of **Dimensions and Expressions**.

2. Select the **Show Partial Sums** checkbox.

3. We usually want to see the total and then analyze how it is composed; so in the **Subtotals** section enable the option to view **Subtotals on Top**.

4. Click on **OK**.

Rule 2 – convert color into data

We have already taken advantage of color in the heat map. In the other tables with mini-charts, we can use the same technique that we learned in *Chapter 2*, *Rank Analysis*, to define a background or text color based on a conditional statement. Alternately, we can use the **Visual Cues** tab.

Let's perform the following steps in the **Chart Properties** window to show the negative profit margins in bold and red text:

1. In the **Visual Cues** tab, select **Profit Margin** in the **Expressions** list.

2. Enter 0 into the **Lower** textbox, and to the right, select the **Bold** checkbox.

3. Click on **OK**.

Profit Margin (USD $)
1,083,211
-37,660
-94,707
135,141
334,288
-6,586
110,020
174,526

The profit margin values that are below zero should now appear in bold and red text.

We must also be careful to verify that the use of a colored background doesn't make the text unreadable. For example, in the heat map, white text is easier to read. Let's change the text color from black to white in the **Chart Properties** window.

1. In the **Visual Cues** tab, select all the metrics at once in the **Expressions** list.

2. Change the color that corresponds to **Normal** from black to white.

3. Click on **OK**.

Rule 3 – add more detail

There is no limit to the number of dimensions and metrics that we can add to a table chart. However, adding more than one dimension to a straight table chart makes it harder to understand. Additionally, adding too many dimensions and expressions extends the time needed to calculate table charts, especially pivot table charts. In some cases, we add a dimensional group to a table chart just as we did in *Chapter 3, Trend Analysis*.

Rule 4 – throw away chartjunk

Along with removal of the print icon from the caption, we eliminate unnecessary numbers and the table grid.

Number format

If the amounts are in the thousands, millions, or billions then decimal numbers are not necessary. Also, we prefer to place the unit of measure in the chart label or column label instead of repeating the unit symbol over and over again for every single numeric value.

Let's perform the following steps to properly format the numbers in the **Chart Properties** window:

1. In the **Numbers** tab, select all the metrics at once in the **Expressions** list in the upper left-hand corner, and select the **Integer** option in the **Number Format Settings** section.
2. Click on **OK**.

Table grid

If the columns are generously spaced apart, we can use space alone to separate the columns.

Let's eliminate the vertical line dividing the column by following the given steps in the **Chart Properties** window:

1. In the **Style** tab, clear the **Vertical Dimension Cell Borders** and **Vertical Expression Cell Borders** checkboxes.
2. In the straight table chart with embedded mini-charts, we help our eyes to keep track of the customer that is associated with each metric by typing 1 in the **Stripes every n Rows** textbox.

3. Click on **OK**.

South Wayne Health Services	685,432			-37,660	
Springdale Dept of Justice	519,388			-94,707	
Pollock Fire Department	498,542			135,141	
City of West Harrison	466,563			334,288	

If spacing is limited, then vertical grid lines may be necessary to divide the columns.

Rule 5 – respect usability

Verify that frequently used caption shortcuts are included in the caption and that the scrollbar is at least 14 points wide.

Whenever possible, we keep the **Drag and Drop** checkbox selected in the **Presentation** tab so that users are able change the order in which the columns appear. Also, we keep the **Interactive Sort** checkbox selected in the **Sort** tab along with the **Sort Indicators** checkbox selected in the **Presentation** tab, so that users can define and see how the table is sorted.

Rule 6 – be honest

The same rules that applied to bar charts and line charts as separate objects apply also to their corresponding mini-charts.

First, we must be careful about the size of the cell that contains the mini-chart. Mini line charts are often too wide and show little movement. We fix this problem by reducing the width of the column containing the mini-chart or increasing the height of the rows by selecting the **Wrap Cell Text** checkbox in the **Presentation** tab.

Second, the option to force a mini-chart axis to zero is found in the **Mini Chart Settings** window. The **Force Zero Based Scaling** checkbox is selected by default.

The final results of our heat map shows a possible relationship between a low profit margin and the number of days worked. Almost every time profit margin is orange, days worked appears in blue as shown in the following screenshot:

Customer KPI Heat Map (blue=high, orange=low)				
Customer	Net Sales (USD $)	Profit Margin (USD $)	Days Worked	Num. of Consultants
South Wayne Health Services	535,346	-71,106	3,985	57
Springdale Dept of Justice	519,388	-94,707	5,546	25
City of West Harrison	435,195	326,558	2,594	22
General Forge and Foundry	308,604	93,042	4,447	38
Industrial Automation	299,385	-49,855	5,257	33
Globex Corporation	248,578	-62,429	2,404	36
Adams Center Animal Control	231,767	125,308	2,217	23
Videlectrix	208,168	133,199	1,598	22
Input, Inc.	194,704	-15,115	3,064	46
Initrode	183,920	9,358	3,434	29
Snead County	183,139	-55,718	5,692	38

Our straight table chart with embedded mini-charts confirms this relationship with the bar chart and shows that the number of days worked continues to increase for customers that are not profitable in the mini line charts as shown in the following screenshot:

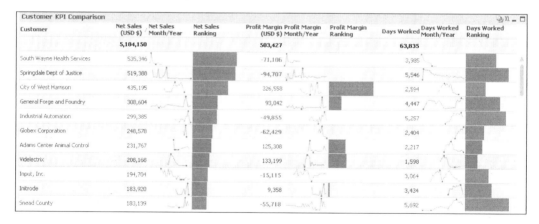

Finally, our pivot table chart with embedded mini-charts quickens our ability to detect large and small numbers in an otherwise plain table as follows:

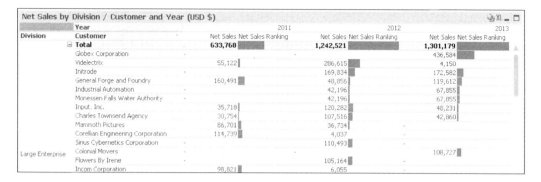

We save our QlikView application before going on to the next chapter.

Summary

Multivariate analysis entails the visualization and analysis of a large number of variables. This analysis method can be implemented by using table charts as a heat map or using mini-charts embedded within table charts. We used the data visualization style guide to make tables easily understandable.

After further analysis, Samantha is more convinced that there is a relationship between the profit or loss a customer contributes to QDataViz, Inc. and the number of days worked for that customer.

We continue our analysis of QDataViz, Inc. and take a closer look at how the number of days worked is distributed between customers using distribution analysis.

5

Distribution Analysis

After four chapters, we dare to wonder if there is any other way to visualize and analyze data besides summing numeric values and segmenting the summed values by predefined dimensions. Let's take a break from the humdrum world of sum and take advantage of underused statistical functions. Samantha doesn't have to be a statistician to use statistical functions and visualization techniques for her benefit.

What is distribution analysis?

Distribution analysis allows us to obtain a greater understanding of a set of numbers. The set of numbers that we use to analyze events is usually a subset of a larger whole. The behavior of this subset can be used to describe the behavior of the whole within a certain margin of error. For example, a subset of past sales can help us to describe all past, present, and future sales.

Samantha likes to know what she can expect from a customer. In how many days will the customer pay? How many days does a data visualization project last? How much does it usually cost to implement a project?

She usually answers these questions by calculating the average of past events. For example, we expect to implement our data visualization projects in 24 days because the average project until now has taken 24 days.

Unfortunately, the average function is overused and abused. In an attempt to simplify analysis, many times we oversimplify and inadvertently distort the data. We've learned in previous chapters that no magical graph answers all of our data visualization needs, and that great analysis involves creating and adjusting charts and perspectives manifold over pertinent data. Similarly, distribution analysis involves using a variety of statistical functions and visualizations that help us to discover new information.

The first method we use to understand a set of numbers involves the chart that best describes its distribution.

Histogram chart

The histogram is a bar chart that is especially designed to show the distributions of a set of numbers. The bars represent how many instances fall into various intervals of numbers defined along the x axis. Our first histogram analyzes the distribution of the number of days our consultants worked for each customer.

To start, we open our QlikView application, copy the **Multivariate Analysis** sheet and rename the new sheet as Distribution Analysis. Finally, we delete the table charts from the **Distribution Analysis** sheet.

Now, we start the process to create a bar chart. When we arrive at the step to define the dimension, we perform the following actions:

1. We want to group the customers into dynamically defined intervals of days worked. Click on **Add Calculated Dimension…** and type the following expression in the **Edit Expression** window:

   ```
   =class(aggr(sum([Days Worked]),Customer),10)
   ```

   The equal sign before the expression is necessary to inform QlikView that the dimension is dynamically defined. Verify that the equal sign is the first character of the expression without any previous spaces.

   Click on **OK**, and then click on **Next >**.

2. The metric is the number of customers in each interval defined by the dimension. Type the following expression in the **Edit Expression** window:

   ```
   count({$<Customer={"=sum([Days Worked])>0"}>} distinct
      Customer)
   ```

3. Click on **Finish**.

We obtain the following chart as a result of the previous exercise. It is a normal bar chart that shows us the number of customers where our consultants have worked between one and ten days, sixty and seventy days, and so on. Each bar represents an interval of the number of days worked, but we can only see intervals that describe the number of days worked for at least one customer.

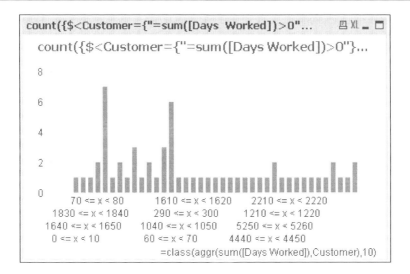

Important functions

Let's take a closer look at the important functions and set analysis we just used before moving on and converting the bar chart into a histogram.

- `class()`: The class function breaks down a list of numbers into intervals or classes. The expression parameter is a field or the resulting list of numbers from a `aggr()` function. The interval parameter defines the size of each and every interval. The syntax for the `class()` function is given as:

  ```
  class(expression, interval [ , label [ , offset ]])
  ```

- `count()`: We first encountered this function in the previous chapter. The `count()` function returns how many table rows of a certain field exist. Table rows that contain a null value in that field are not counted. The distinct keyword is used to return how many of those table rows contain an unique value. The syntax for the `count()` function is given as:

  ```
  count([{set_expression}][ distinct ] [ total [<fld {, fld}>]]
    expression)
  ```

Advanced searches in set analysis

In previous chapters we used fixed text or numeric values to define a set. For example, we used `<Year={'2013'}>` to calculate 2013 net sales.

We can also use an expression and perform an advanced search to define our set. For example, the set definition `<Customer={"=sum([Days Worked])>0"}>` filters out the customers that have zero or less days of work assigned to them.

 When we use an advanced search to filter expressions, we use the QlikView search engine. We can call the QlikView search engine by placing the expression between double quotes (`""`).

The histogram specific properties

In order for a histogram to show number distribution effectively, the ranges should be ordered and space should be left blank for ranges that don't contain any instances. We can perform the following steps to convert a bar chart into a histogram within the **Chart Properties** window:

1. In the **Sort** tab, select the **Numeric Value** checkbox in the **Sort by** section. Select the **Ascending** option in the drop-down box to the right.

2. In the **Axes** tab, select the **Continuous** checkbox in the **Dimension Axis** section.

3. Click on **OK**.

We will now have the following histogram chart:

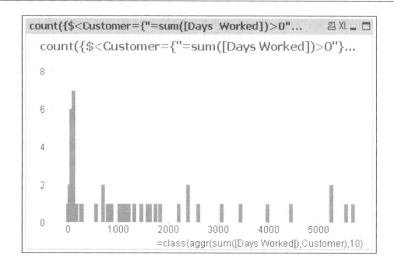

Objects to support histogram charts

Alongside the listboxes, the search object and the current selections object, we add an input box that can easily change the size of the histogram's intervals.

We cannot always be sure of the best interval size that should be used when analyzing a distribution, and we don't want to change the dimension expression every time we change the interval size. As a result, we are going to create a variable that we can change quickly and easily in an **input box**.

The input box

Let's follow the given steps to create a variable and an input box that modifies the variable:

1. Click on **Create Input Box** ⊟ in the design toolbar.
2. Click on **New Variable**.
3. Define the **Variable Name** as vNum_DaysWorkedInterval.
4. Click on the new variable in the **Displayed Variables** list and change the **Label** to Days Worked Interval.
5. Click on **OK**.

Now, let's link the variable to the calculated dimension in the histogram **Chart Properties** window:

1. In the **Dimensions** tab, click on **Edit...**.

2. In the expression, replace 10 with vNum_DaysWorkedInterval. The resulting expression should be as follows:

```
=class(aggr(sum([Days Worked]),[Customer]),
  vNum_DaysWorkedInterval)
```

3. Click on **OK** twice.

Test the link by typing 100 to the right of the equal sign in the input box. Press *Enter* to assign the value to the variable and verify that the histogram displays a different distribution.

Data visualization style guide for histogram charts

Although the histogram chart is based on the bar chart, its data visualization style guide contains different rules.

Rule 1 – use adequate labeling

All components of a chart should be made coherent by adequate labeling. We will use **Tahoma** as the font of all labels and use a font size between **8** and **10**.

In the same manner as we defined the bar chart's labels, define the following labels for the histogram:

Label	Text
Chart	**Distribution of days worked by customer**
Dimension	**Days Worked**
Metric	**# Customers**
Axes label	**# Customers**

We take note that the histogram, unlike many bar charts, has a continuous x axis. We format the numbers along the x axis in the **Number** tab of the **Chart Properties** window. In the **Expressions** list, select **Continuous X-axis** and select the **Integer** option.

Dimensional reference lines

We can add reference lines and text to any chart. We will use reference lines in our histogram chart to understand how common statistical functions can describe the distribution of the days worked by customer.

In the **Chart Properties** window, let's add the reference lines that represent mean (average), median, and two fractiles in our histogram.

1. In the **Presentation** tab, click on **Add...** in the **Reference Lines** section.

2. In the **Label** textbox, type Mean and select the **Show Label in Chart** checkbox.

3. In the **Definition** section, type the following expression in the **Expression** textbox:

```
Avg(aggr(sum({$<Customer={"=sum([Days Worked])>0"}>}
    [Days Worked]),Customer))
```

 We note that the average is calculated with the same set analysis that we used to calculate the metric of the histogram.

4. In the **Line Formatting** section, change the color of the reference line to black and the select a solid line in the **Style** drop-down box.

5. Click on **OK**.

6. Repeat steps from 1 to 5 to draw a red, solid line representing median. Use the following expression:

```
Median(aggr(sum({$<Customer={"=sum([Days Worked])>0"}>}
    [Days Worked]),Customer))
```

7. Repeat steps from 1 to 5 to draw a blue, dotted line representing the 1/10 fractile. Do not show the label in the chart. Use the following expression:

```
Fractile(aggr(sum({$<Customer={"=sum([Days Worked])>0"}>}
    [Days Worked]),Customer),.1)
```

8. Repeat steps from 1 to 5 to draw a blue, dotted line representing the 9/10 fractile. Do not show the label in the chart. Use the following expression:

```
Fractile(aggr(sum({$<Customer={"=sum([Days Worked])>0"}>} ,
    [Days Worked]),Customer),.9)
```

9. Click on **OK**.

We now have the following histogram with four reference lines and adequate labeling:

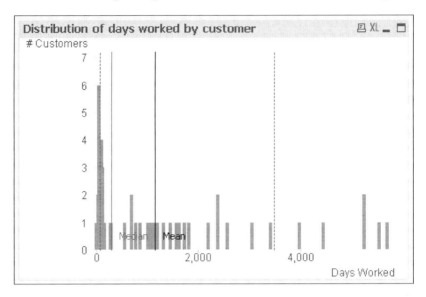

Important functions

Let's review the important functions that we just used in the previous exercise.

- `avg ([{set_expression}] [ distinct ] [ total [<fld {,fld}>]` `] expression )`: The `avg()` function returns the mean of a set of numeric values. The mean is defined as the sum of all numeric values divided by the number of numeric values.

- `median ([{set_expression}] [ distinct ] [ total [<fld {,fld}>]` `] expression )`: The `median()` function returns the numeric value that is both greater and less than 50 percent of the numeric values in a set. If there is an even number of numeric values in a set, the median is the mean of the two middle numeric values.

- `fractile ([{set_expression}] [ distinct ] [ total [<fld {,fld}>] ] expression, fractile):` function will return the numeric value that is greater than a certain fraction of the numeric values in a set. For example, if the fractile is 0.25, the numeric value that is returned is greater than 25 percent of the numeric values in the set. The fractiles of 0.25 and 0.75 are called **quartiles** and the fractile of 0.5 is the **median**. Although mean is the most common measure to describe the distribution of numeric values, it is susceptible to **outliers**, or extreme values far greater or far smaller than most of the numeric values in the set. Outliers can distort the mean value so much that the mean can be greater than 90 percent of the numeric values in a set, and therefore, be the basis for incorrect interpretations and predictions. As a result, we recommend using the median and fractiles to complement the mean.

Rule 2 – convert color into data

Color is not so important for histograms because the data is homogenous. It is important that the bars' color doesn't interfere with the reference lines and their labels hard to see.

Rather than using reference lines, we can also identify bars that contain the median and fractile values by highlighting them. We learned this coloring technique in *Chapter 2, Rank Analysis*.

Rule 3 – add more detail

Similar to a bar chart, a histogram is a great candidate to be converted into a trellis chart. However, there are two additional methods for adding more detail to a distribution analysis.

Frequency polygon

A frequency polygon is a line chart that compares various distributions in the same chart. Before creating a frequency polygon, let's follow the given steps to learn an alternate way to clone a chart:

1. With the *Ctrl* key pressed, left-click on the caption of our current histogram and drag the mouse away from the original chart. We should now have two histograms.

2. In the **Chart Properties** window of the cloned histogram, rename the chart as Distribution of days worked by customer and division.

Now, let's continue the process to create a frequency polygon and follow the given steps in the **Chart Properties** window of the cloned histogram:

1. In the **General** tab, change **Chart Type** to **Line Chart**.
2. In the **Dimension** tab, add Division to the **Used Dimensions** list.
3. In the **Expressions** tab, select the **Symbol** checkbox.

> We notice later that the line drawn by QlikView never indicates when an interval contains zero customers. QlikView draws a straight line from one interval that has at least one customer to the next interval with at least one customer. Although not a perfect solution, we add symbols to recognize which intervals have customers and which are empty.

4. To avoid clutter, remove the reference lines in the **Presentation** tab. Select each reference line and click on **Delete**.
5. Click on **OK**.

The resulting chart resembles the following screenshot where we can compare the distribution of each division:

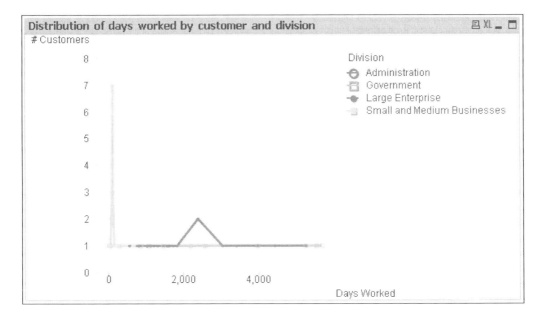

We notice that the customers of the **Small and Medium Businesses** division are located on the left-hand side of the distribution while the customers of the **Government** and **Large Enterprise** divisions are evenly distributed to the right. This type of segmentation may help us to estimate the number of days we expect to work for any customer.

As a line chart, the frequency polygon is limited by how many segments it can effectively display. Therefore, when we want to divide a distribution into more than seven segments, we use a box plot chart.

Box plot

Earlier in the chapter, we created reference lines in the histogram to understand the relationship between the different statistical measures and the actual distribution of the numeric values they represent. A box plot represents a of a histogram using those key statistical measures. We use the median, the 0.25 fractile (lower quartile), the 0.75 fractile (upper quartile), the minimum and the maximum values to summarize the distribution of a segmented set of numeric values. A sample box plot is displayed in the following diagram:

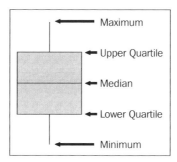

We will use the **Box Plot Wizard** to create a box plot chart.

1. In the **Tools** menu, click on **Box Plot Wizard**.
2. Click on **Next >**.
3. Select **Project Name** in the **Dimension** drop-down box.
4. Select **Customer** in the **Aggregator** drop-down box.
5. Type the following expression in the **Expression** textbox:
   ```
   sum({$<Customer={"=sum([Days Worked])>0"}>} [Days Worked])
   ```
6. Click on **Next >**.
7. Select **Median mode** in the **Display Mode** drop-down box.

The **Average mode** creates a box plot chart using the mean instead of the median and standard deviations instead of quartiles. A box plot chart based on the median and quartiles is more reliable and easier to understand.

8. Click on **Finish**.

9. After we apply adequate labeling, we obtain the following box plot chart:

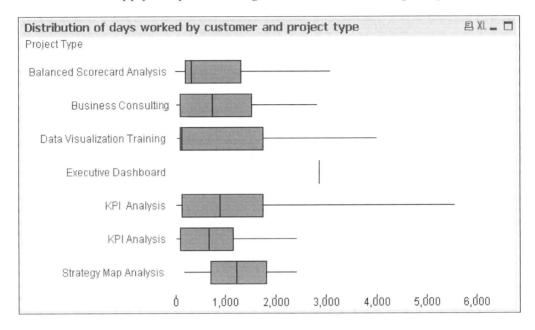

This type of chart is great for visualizing, comparing, and then predicting the number of days needed for each project type. In a different scenario with different data, a box plot chart can help us estimate how long a vendor will take to deliver certain goods or how long we have to wait for a customer payment.

Rule 4 – throw away chartjunk

Almost all the ink in the histogram is used for data or usability. As with previous charts, we recommend removing the print icon from the caption.

Rule 5 – respect usability

Similar to the bar chart, verify the usability within the following areas of the chart object:

Area	Options
Caption	*Add the shortcut that copies the chart's image to the clipboard*
Inside the chart	*Widen the scrollbar to 14 points*

Rule 6 – be honest

A common mistake when dealing with histograms is to create intervals that are not consistent. For example, when the maximum value is far from the center, we may be tempted to make a histogram with intervals of 0-5, 5-10, 10-25, 25-50, 50-100, and above 100. Inconsistent intervals distort the distribution and can prevent potential discoveries.

 Always create histograms that use consistently sized intervals.

As long as the size of the interval is consistent, we can use intervals of 5, 10, or 100. While larger intervals hide the distribution peaks that can be used to detect subgroups, smaller intervals may appear chaotic and unintelligible. There does not exist any perfect interval size, so the best analysis technique we offer is to allow for an easy way to quickly change the interval's size.

We save our QlikView application before going on to the next chapter.

Summary

Distribution analysis provides a different perspective of our data and raises the possibility of discovering something new. This analysis method can be done using a histogram, a frequency polygon, a box plot, or certain statistical measures.

After applying the data visualization style guide, Samantha discovers that the number of days worked by customer varies widely, but no customer stands out as having consumed an excessive amount of days. This is especially true when segmenting the histogram by division and noting the similarity between each segment's median and mean value. We still haven't found anything substantial that explains why some projects generate a loss for QDataViz, Inc.

Let's continue and look at ways in which Samantha can discover whether a relationship exists between two variables with correlation analysis.

6

Correlation Analysis

When analyzing data, we are constantly looking for the causes and effects of certain events. Discovering a causal relationship between events is significant because we can take action upon it. If the effect is beneficial, we will promote what causes it; however, if the effect is detrimental, we will discourage the cause. Correlation analysis will help us discover the relationships between metrics. Then, it is up to us to apply human intuition to determine if they are causal relationships.

What is correlation analysis?

Samantha notes that several projects have incurred losses. What other events coincide with those losses? Could one of the other events be the cause? What is the effect of these losses on QDataViz, Inc.'s financial health?

The losses might have been caused by some descriptive value such as the poor selling practices of a particular salesperson. We could have formed this hypothesis after viewing a simple bar chart that displays profit margins by salesperson.

However, what if Samantha wants to test if losses are related to, and possibly caused by, another metric? If project losses are correlated to the number of external consultants involved in the project, the number of days budgeted for the project, or the number of sunny days during the project then we can recognize this perfectly using a scatterplot chart.

Samantha uses a scatterplot chart to discover a possible relationship, but it is up to her to decide if the relationship is either causal, a related effect of the same cause or purely coincidental. For example, the number of external consultants could be a cause of project losses that could be avoided if more internal consultants were used. Project losses and the number of days budgeted could be a shared symptom of poor project scoping methods. Finally, a relationship between the number of sunny days during the project and project losses is complete coincidence since no outdoor activities are involved.

Samantha will use both visual cues and mathematical methods to prove or disprove relationships between metrics.

Scatterplot chart

The scatterplot chart involves plotting a symbol that represents two different metrics along an x axis and y axis.

To start, we open our QlikView application, copy the **Distribution Analysis** sheet and rename the new sheet `Correlation Analysis`. Finally, we delete the distribution analysis charts from the **Correlation Analysis** sheet.

We want to analyse the relationship between the number of days worked for a project and project margin, so let's create a chart with the following characteristics:

Type of chart	Scatter chart (shown in the previous image)
Dimension	[Project Code]
First metric	sum([Days Worked])
Second metric	sum([Profit Margin])

Note that the **Expressions** window is different for scatterplot charts. The chart wizard reminds us that a scatterplot must have at least two metrics: one metric along the x-axis and one metric along the y-axis. Optionally, we can include a third metric along a z-axis that refers to the size of the dot and not an actual third axis.

In the scatterplot's **Expressions** window, we create the chart defined in the previous table by selecting `Days Worked` in the **X** drop-down box and `Profit Margin` in the **Y** drop-down box. QlikView automatically assumes that the values will be summed.

 Select the **Advanced Mode** checkbox to view the normal **Expressions** window. The first metric corresponds to the x-axis and the second to the y-axis.

We now have the following scatterplot chart:

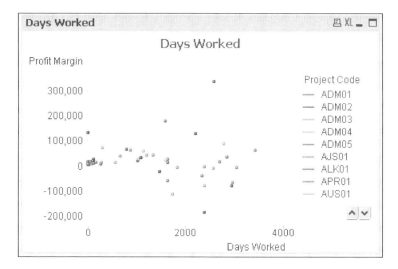

Data visualization style guide for scatterplot charts

The scatterplot chart contains several new items to consider in our data visualization style guide. We take the time to review a few previous rules and add some new ones.

Rule 1: use adequate labeling

All components of a chart should be made coherent by adequate labeling. We will use **Tahoma** as the font of all labels and use font size **8** to **10**.

Define the following labels as we've discussed in previous chapters:

Label	Text
Chart	`Days worked vs. project margin by project`
Dimension	`Project Code`
Metric	`Profit Margin` and `Days Worked`
Axes label	`K` as the **Thousand Symbol**

Finally, verify that the number format of each expression is `Integer` in the **Numbers** tab and add a reference line at `0` in the **Presentation** tab.

Trendlines

Trendlines play an important role in visualizing the strength of the relationship between two metrics in a scatterplot. A trendline, or a linear regression, is basically the average of all the plotted dots. The closer all the dots are to the average, the stronger the relationship is between the two metrics.

The correlation can be positive or negative, weak or strong. Often, no correlation exists between two metrics. Rarely are real correlations so simple as the following example correlations, so we draw a linear regression to help determine how two metrics are related, if at all. The following figure shows a few example correlations:

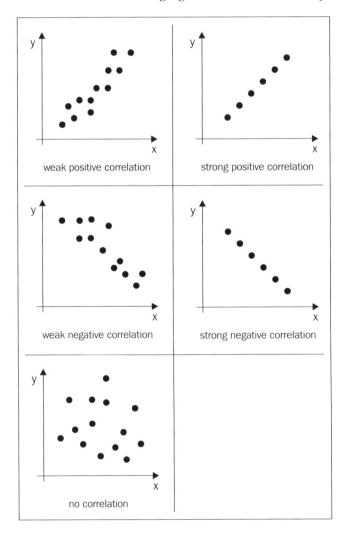

We add a linear regression to a scatterplot chart by the following steps:

1. Right-click on the scatterplot chart and select **Properties...**
2. In the **Expression** tab, select the **Advanced Mode** checkbox.
3. Select the second expression, `Profit Margin`, and select the **Linear** checkbox in the **Trendlines** section.
4. Additionally, select the **Show Equation** and **Show R2** checkboxes in the same **Trendlines** section.
5. Click on **OK**.

After adding adequate labeling and a linear regression, we obtain the following chart:

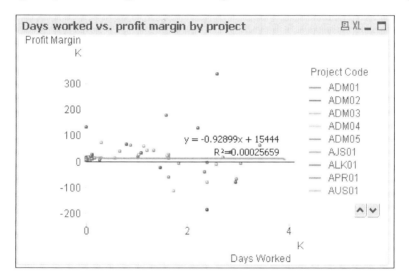

The equation represents the line. If the relationship between the two metrics was strong, then that equation would help us estimate the profit margin based solely on the number of days worked.

 The independent variable or possible cause is placed on the x-axis and the dependent variable or possible effect is placed on the y-axis.

The strength of the relationship between the two metrics is represented by the value of R2. An R2 of 1 means that the relationship between the two metrics is well-defined while an R2 of 0 means that no relation exists between the two metrics. Usually, the R2 value falls between 0 and 1, so the closer the value is to 1, the more well-defined the relationship is.

According to the previous chart, no correlation exists between the number of days worked for a project and the project's profit margin. This is not what Samantha expected. Ideally, as the number of days worked increases, so should the project margin. Let's see how we can add more data to our scatterplot chart to solve this mystery.

Rule 2 – convert color into data

We use color to group the plotted dots in the chart and analyze whether stronger relationships exist within those groups. Groups that have a correlation greater than the whole are called clusters.

Before we begin, clone the **Days worked vs. project margin by project chart** and rename the new chart `Days worked vs. profit margin by project (Grouped by division)`.

Perform the following steps in the **Chart Properties** window of the cloned chart:

1. In the **Expressions** tab, expand the **Days Worked** expression.
2. Select **Background Color** and click on **...** in the **Definition** textbox.
3. Type the following code in the **Edit Expression** window:

```
=pick(wildmatch(Division, 'Government','LargeEnterprise','Small
and Medium Businesses','*')
,Red()
,LightBlue()
,Black()
,LightGray()
)
```

4. Click OK.

Since the dots are solid spheres, some dots could hide others that are located below them. We can minimize this defect if we change the dots into crosses in the **Chart Properties** window.

1. In the **Style** tab, select the option that includes crosses in the **Look** section.
2. In the **Presentation** tab, set the **Symbol Size** to **3pt**.
3. Click on **OK**.

An alternative solution to prevent dots from hiding under others is to make their colors transparent.

After removing the linear regression, we can analyze whether the projects grouped by their corresponding divisions create clusters within the scatterplot chart as shown in the following figure:

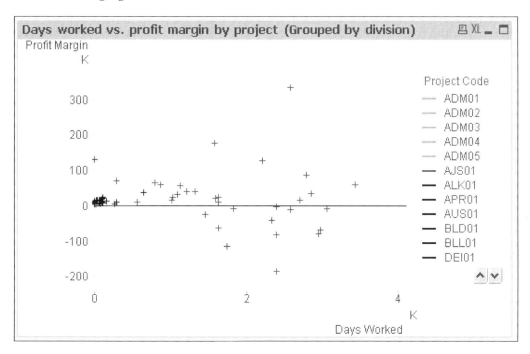

Important function

Let's take a closer look at the powerful function we recently used in the previous exercise before moving on to the next rule.

- pick(n, expr1[, expr2,...exprN]): The `pick()` function saves time and space. The following `if` statement works perfectly: if(x=1,'a', if(x=2, 'b')).However, it is much easier and more elegant to write `pick(x, 'a', 'b')`.This is especially the case when the if-statement is extensive. The `wildmatch()` function used in the exercise works well with the `pick()` function because it returns the number that corresponds with the position of the string that matches the field value. For example, if the **Division** value being evaluated is `Large Enterprise` then `wildmatch(Division, 'Government','LargeEnterpris e','Small and Medium Businesses','*')`returns 2. The `pick()` function then uses that 2 to return its second expression.

Rule 3 – add more detail

Like previous charts, a scatterplot chart is a great candidate to convert into a trellis chart. We can also add more detail using the following methods:

- Z axis
- Trails
- Animation

Z axis

The Z axis in QlikView corresponds to the size of the dot instead of a third axis.

Before we add the Z axis, clone the **Days worked vs. profit margin by project (Grouped by division)** chart and rename the new chart as `Days worked vs. profit margin vs. days worked by external consultants by project (Grouped by division)`.

Perform the following steps in the **Chart Properties** window of the cloned chart:

1. In the **Expression** tab, click on **Add**.
2. Type `sum({$<[Employee Type] = {'External'}>} [Days Worked])` in the **Edit Expression** window.
3. Label the new metric as `Days Worked by External Consultants` in the **Expressions** tab and define it as an **Integer** in the **Number** tab.
4. In the **Style** tab, change the style to hollow circles of varying sizes.
5. Click on **OK**.

If the circle grows bigger as the values on the x axis and y axis increase or decrease, then we could be visualizing some kind of relationship between the three metrics. We can confirm this by creating two other scatterplots that compare the first and third metrics and then the second and third metrics. The result of our previous exercise is shown in the following figure:

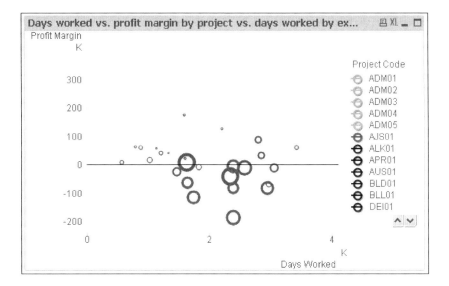

Samantha notices that as the profit margin decreases, the number of days worked by external consultants increases. She creates an additional scatterplot chart to confirm her observation and discovers a negative correlation between days worked by external consultants and the profit margin. Her scatterplot chart displayed in the following chart is filtered to show only the **Large Enterprise** division:

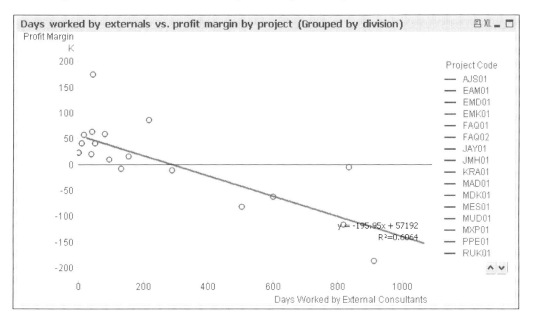

Trails

Surprisingly, it is possible to use a scatterplot to show the changes of a correlation over time. The first way to display change is to show the path a dot has traveled over time.

Before we add trails, clone the **Days worked vs. profit margin vs. days worked by external consultants by project (Grouped by division)** chart and rename the new chart Days worked vs. profit margin vs. days worked by external consultants by project over time trails (Grouped by division).

Perform the following steps in the **Chart Properties** window of the cloned chart:

1. In the **Dimension** tab, remove Project Code from the **Used Dimensions List** and add Year and Division. Year should be first in the list of **Used Dimensions**.

2. In the **Presentation** tab, select the **Show Arrows** checkbox and increase the **Arrow Size** to 3pt.

3. Click on **OK**.

We change the dimension from Project Code to Division because too many trails makes the scatterplot chart unintelligible. Now we can see in the following figure how the relationship by division has evolved over the past three years:

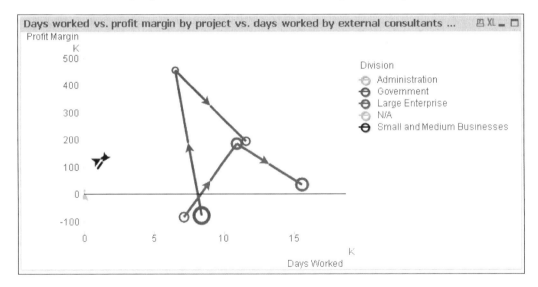

Animation

Hans Rosling is famous for his animated presentations at Technology, Entertainment, Design (TED) conferences where he tells stories with animated scatterplot charts. Each frame of the animated scatterplot chart is a photo of that chart at a certain moment in time.

Before we add animation, clone the **Days worked vs. profit margin vs. days worked by external consultants by project over time trails (Grouped by division)** chart and rename the new chart `Days worked vs. profit margin vs. days worked by external consultants by project over animated time (Grouped by division)`.

Perform the following steps in the **Chart Properties** window of the cloned chart:

1. In the **Dimensions** tab, click on **Animate...** in the lower, left-hand corner.
2. Select the **Animate the First Dimension** and the **Show Animation Dimension Value** checkboxes.
3. In the **Alignment** section, select **Centered** in the **Horizontal** drop-down box.
4. Click on **Font...** and change the font to **Tahoma** and the size to **24**. Click on **OK**.
5. Click on **OK** twice.

Our scatterplot now includes a play button that animates the chart. Animation creates less clutter than trails, and as such, can handle more dots. The scatterplot is shown in the following figure:

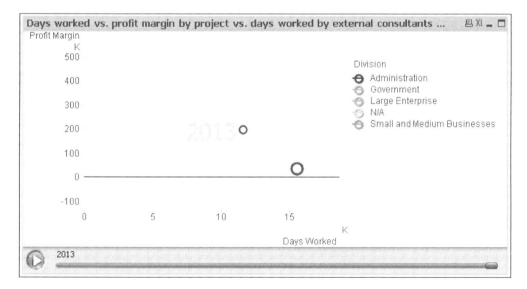

Rule 4 – throw away chartjunk

Almost all the ink in the scatterplot chart is used for data or usability. Like previous charts, we recommend removing the print icon from the caption.

If the dots plotted in the scatterplot chart number more than fifteen, displaying the legend is useless and wasteful. We can remove the legend in the **Presentation** tab of the **Chart Properties** window.

Rule 5 – respect usability

Like the previous chart, verify the usability within the following areas of the chart object:

Area	Options
Caption	*Add the shortcut that copies the chart's image to the clipboard*

Rule 6 – be honest

The scatterplot is better viewed when both axes have the same length. Redistribute the area used by the chart and other components by holding down *Crtl+Shift* and adjusting the red lines that appear within the chart object.

We save our QlikView application before going on to the next chapter.

Summary

Correlation analysis can be used to detect relationships between different metrics. The type of relationship (cause and effect, common symptom, or coincidence) is up to Samantha to decide given her knowledge of QDataViz, Inc.

After conducting her analysis, she has come to the conclusion that the number of external consultants assigned to a project greatly affects its profitability. Before moving on to finding a possible solution, let's look at how we can analyze our data geographically and discover where we are using external consultants.

7
Geographical Analysis

In everyday life, we frequently analyze maps to understand our current location and how to get from point A to point B. We also regularly view maps that include other superimposed data such as temperature, atmospheric conditions, elevation, vegetation, political boundaries, and demographics. We would be foolish to overlook using geographical analysis for our own data.

What is geographical analysis?

Samantha wants to compare the geographic locations of the customers where external consultants work. In other scenarios, we could also use geographical analysis to find potential customers by comparing the location and demographics of our current sales with other locations of the same demographic characteristics. We could investigate our supply chain and compare the locations of our suppliers, warehouses, and customers. We could also create a custom map that is a floor plan of a shopping mall and analyze if sales are greater in stores located near the movie theatre.

Samantha is interested in creating an area map chart. An area map chart uses color and areas, such as countries, states, or zip codes to display information. In order to add a map chart to QlikView, we are going to introduce **QlikMarket** and download a map chart extension that provides a chart type not available by default in QlikView.

QlikMarket

QlikMarket offers industry-specific and department-specific templates, demos of products that integrate with QlikView and custom extensions that expand QlikView's default functionality. IdevioMaps, GeoQlik, and Esri can be integrated with QlikView and provide robust geographical analysis. For the additional cost of these tools, we are able to manage larger volumes of data and create more complex visualizations that include geographical heat maps and mini-chart overlays.

However, we can also download a free extension provided by QlikTech, the maker of QlikView, that offers a simple area map chart. **Extensions** are custom charts anybody can develop and integrate with QlikView. If we want to use an extension, we have to download and install it manually.

We download the QlikView SVG Map extension at `http://market.qlikview.com/qlikview-svg-map.html`. We install the extension by opening the downloaded zip file and double-clicking `svgMap.qar`. When we double-click on the `.qar` file, QlikView opens and we receive a message confirming the installation as shown in the following screenshot:

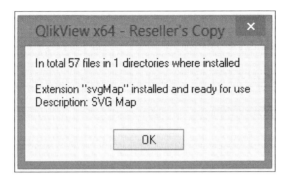

Area map chart

We cannot work with extensions in QlikView's normal interface. We have to enable QlikView's AJAX interface to add an extension to our QlikView application.

Let's copy the **Correlation Analysis** sheet, rename it `Geographical Analysis` and delete the scatterplot charts to make room for our first extension object. We follow the next given steps to create the area map chart:

1. Click on **Turn on/off WebView** in the design toolbar.
2. Right-click over any blank space in the sheet and select **New Sheet Object**.
3. In the **New Sheet Object** window, select **Extension Objects**.
4. Left-click and drag the **SVG Map** object into the sheet.
5. Right-click on the new object and select **Properties...**

Although the interface is different, we still have to choose which dimensions and metrics compose the chart.

Dimensions

The dimension is defined in the **Region ID** drop-down box. The field must contain ISO codes that represent the areas defined in the map we select in the **Map** drop-down box. In the case of the United States, the field defined as **Region ID** must contain either two-character long state abbreviations or the **Federal Information Processing Standards (FIPS)** code.

ISO codes: `http://en.wikipedia.org/wiki/ISO_3166-2`
FIPS codes: `http://en.wikipedia.org/wiki/Federal_Information_Processing_Standard_state_code`

QDataViz, Inc.'s customers are located in the United States, so we select **Customer_State** in the **Region_ID** drop-down box and **US** in the **Map** drop-down box.

Metrics

Further down the **Properties** window, we have to option to include a metric in the **Measure** textbox. The larger the result of the measure, the darker the shade of the color that paints the region. To avoid extreme shading, we divide the number of days worked in each state by the greatest number of days worked in any state. As such, we expect the result to be between zero and one hundred.

Type the following expression into the **Measure** textbox:

```
=sum({$<[Employee Type] = {'External'}>} [Days Worked])
/
Max(total aggr(sum({$<[Employee Type] = {'External'}>} [Days Worked])
, [Customer_State]))
*100
```

The `total` keyword allows the `max()` function to calculate the maximum value of any customer regardless of the dimension value in the chart.

We also define the regions' base color in the **Color Expression** textbox. The color can be based on certain conditions, but it must always be defined in hexagonal format. We can search for a color in hexagonal format using any color wheel found on the Internet. ColorExplorer (`http://colorexplorer.com/colorpicker.aspx`) is one example.

Type the following expression into the **Color Expression** text box.

```
='#397DAB'
```

Finally, in the **Popup Contents** textbox, we define the text that appears in the popup window when we hover over a region. The text is defined by concatenating QlikView functions with HTML tags.

Type the following expression into the **Popup Contents** textbox:

```
='<strong>' &[Customer_State]& '</strong><br />' &sum({$<[Employee
Type] = {'External'}>} [Days Worked])
```

The area map chart updates as we modify its properties, so we don't have to click on **Finish** or **OK**. We exit the **Properties** window by clicking **X** in the top, right-hand corner of the window.

The following chart helps Samantha recognize any regions that use more external consultants than others.

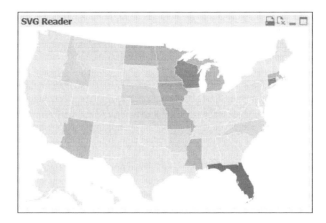

Data visualization style guide for area map charts

Lets' briefly review the data visualization rules for area map charts.

Rule 1 – use adequate labeling

All components of a chart should be made coherent by adequate labeling. We will use **Tahoma** as the font of all labels and use font size **8** to **10**.

We've already seen how to add pop ups. Now, let's define the chart's label in the **Caption** tab within the extension's **Properties** window. We name the chart Days worked by external consultants by state.

Rule 2 – convert color into data

Color is a vital component of an area map chart. We create color blind safe maps if we select just one color and view the data using shades of that same color.

Nevertheless, if we want to add conditions, we can find color blind safe color schemes at `http://colorbrewer2.org/` and follow the next given steps to add the color scheme to the map:

1. Right-click on the area map chart and click on **Copy**.
2. Right-click over any empty area in the sheet and click on **Paste Sheet Object**.
3. In the **What do you want to do?** window, select **Create a copy**.
4. Drag the new chart object away from the original chart.
5. Right-click on the new chart and select **Properties...**
6. In the **Caption** tab, change the **Label** to External consultants and profit margin by state (Conditional color scheme).
7. Type the following values into their corresponding text boxes:

Text Box	Value

Measure	`=fabs(sum([Profit`
	`    Margin])/sum([Net`
	`    Sales]))`

Color expression	`=if(`
	`    sum([Profit`
	`        Margin])/sum([Net`
	`        Sales]) < 0,`
	`        '#FC8D59',`
	`        if(`
	`            sum([Profit`
	`            Margin])/sum([Net`
	`            Sales]) > .2,`
	`            '#91BFDB',`
	`            '#FFFFBF'`
	`        )`
	`    )`

Popup contents	`='<strong>' &` `    [Customer_State] &` `    '</strong> ' & sum([Profit` `    Margin])/sum([Net` `    Sales])`

8. Click on **X**.

Finally, make sure the **Disabled Color** in the **Properties** window doesn't conflict with any of the colors that show data.

 The expression defined in the **Measure** textbox controls the shade of the color drawn on the map. The fabs() function makes all values positive. This causes the orange to darken as negative profit margins decrease. Otherwise, the orange would lighten as negative profit margins decrease.

The following chart uses orange to encode negative profit margin, yellow to encode low, positive profit margin, and blue to encode high, positive profit margin. The color's shade encodes the magnitude of the negative and positive profit margins.

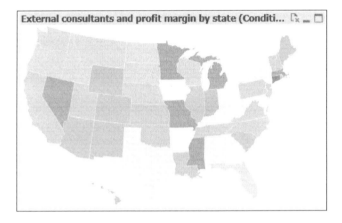

If we view this area map chart alongside the original area map chart, we notice that the profit margin is low where the number of days worked by external consultants is high.

Rule 3 – add more detail

If we want to add more detail by overlaying mini charts, symbols, or icons, we would look into purchasing a more robust geographical analysis tools such as IdevioMaps, GeoQlik, and Esri.

Rule 4 – throw away chartjunk

Like previous charts, we recommend removing the print icon from the caption. We disable this option in the **Properties** window by clicking **More...** in the **Caption** tab and clearing the **Print** checkbox.

If we add overlaying icons, we avoid adding cartoonish stoplights and art that detracts from the original area map chart.

Rule 5 – respect usability

Along with verifying the caption shortcuts, review the usability within the chart. In the **Properties** window, we can test two options: **Zoom Selected Regions** and **Show Controls**.

Rule 6 – be honest

Geographical analysis has been the victim of terrible misinterpretations throughout the years. For example, teachers using flattened world maps struggle to explain that Greenland isn't the size of most of North America, or the same size as South America or Africa. Though not a perfect solution, we use elliptical global maps when necessary. Luckily, regional and country maps are less susceptible to this problem, but we are always careful to consider whether the areas in the map are correctly displayed.

We save our QlikView application before going on to the next chapter.

Summary

Geographical analysis is part of our everyday lives, and it can be an important aspect of our data discovery experience. We recommend browsing QlikMarket to see how to expand on QlikView's default functionality.

Now, let's look at possible solutions to QDataViz, Inc.'s problems by using what-if analysis.

8

What-if Analysis

In previous chapters we focused on analyzing data from QDataViz, Inc.'s customer invoice and project management system. However, Samantha is also an important source of information. She supplies her own data through custom variables and then studies alternate outcomes of past events by mixing them with the historical data. In this manner, she can also analyze possible future results.

What is what-if analysis?

Samantha wonders what would have happened to each project's profit margin if external consultants had worked fewer days. Also, what if internal consultants replaced the external ones and worked the same amount of days or more? What if the cost of internal consultants was to rise as a result of more aggressive recruitment efforts? The answers to these questions would help us to discover possible solutions to our problem.

Unlike previous analysis techniques, what-if analysis doesn't incorporate any particular data visualization. We can effectively use what-if analysis on top of any other analysis or data visualization technique.

What-if analysis involves three steps as follows: creating independent variables whose values Samantha can modify, integrating the variables with historical data, and comparing the real outcome with an alternate one. The independent variables can either be global or detailed.

Global variable what-if analysis

The global variable what-if analysis method is a simple, quick solution that has little impact on our QlikView application's performance.

In `Sales_Project_Analysis_Sandbox.qvw`, let's copy the **Geographical Analysis** sheet, rename it as `What-if Analysis` and delete the area map charts to make room our what-if analysis.

Let's create a chart called **What-if Consultant Cost / Profit by Customer** with the following characteristics:

Type of chart	Straight table
Dimension	Customer
First metric (Profit)	sum([Profit Margin])
Second metric (External Consultant Cost)	sum({< [Employee Type]={'External'}>} [Cost of Sales] * [Days Worked])
Third metric (Internal Consultant Cost)	sum({< [Employee Type]={'Internal'}>} [Cost of Sales] * [Days Worked])

Here, we use the topics learned in *Chapter 4, Multivariate Analysis*, to produce the following table:

What-if Consultant Cost / Profit by Customer			
Customer	Profit	External Consultant Cost	Internal Consultant Cost
	1,055,505	**2,582,510**	**2,097,106**
Corellian Engineering Corporation	-187,757	254,200	52,332
Charles Townsend Agency	-116,194	247,356	49,967
Springdale Dept of Justice	-94,707	448,359	165,735
Smith and Co.	-63,769	149,492	40,788
Snead County	-55,718	57,919	180,938
Industrial Automation	-49,855	184,666	164,573
South Wayne Health Services	-34,578	558,736	47,717
City of Bunnell	-25,670	61,722	49,845
Input, Inc.	-10,977	88,654	121,166
Foo Bars	-9,602	33,960	58,552
Globex Corporation	-4,513	248,411	62,596
McMahon and Tate	3,190	0	7,935
Megadodo Publications	4,364	0	0

Global variables

Let's create two new global variables and integrate them with the preceding chart.

1. In the **Settings** menu, select **Variable Overview...**.

2. Click on **Add**.

3. In the **New Variable** textbox, type `vPct_ExternalConsultantCostChange`.

4. Click on **OK**.

5. Again, click on **Add**.

6. In the **New Variable** textbox, type `vPct_InternalConsultantCostChange`.

7. Click on **OK** twice.

8. Click on **Create Input Box** ▣ in the design toolbar.

9. Double-click on **vPct_ExternalConsultantCostChange** and **vPct_InternalConsultantCostChange** in the **Available Variables** list.

10. Select **vPct_ExternalConsultantCostChange** in the **Displayed Variables** list and change **Label** to **% External Consultant Cost Change**.

11. Select **vPct_InternalConsultantCostChange** in the **Displayed Variables** list and change **Label** to **% Internal Consultant Cost Change**.

12. Click on **OK**.

We now have two new global variables and an input box to assign them values. Finally, let's go to the **Chart Properties** window of the **What-if Consultant Cost / Profit by Customer** chart and add the following metrics that make reference to the new variables:

Metric label	Metric expression

Profit (What-if)	`sum([Net Sales])-`
	
	`sum({<[Product Type] = {'Licenses','Maintenance'}>} [Cost of Sales])-`
	
	`sum({<[Employee Type]={'External'}>} [Cost of Sales] * [Days Worked]) * (1+vPct_ExternalConsultantCostChange)-`
	
	`sum({<[Employee Type]={'Internal'}>} [Cost of Sales] * [Days Worked]) * (1+vPct_InternalConsultantCostChange)`

Metric label	Metric expression
External Consultant Cost (What-if)	```sum({<[Employee Type]={'External'}>} [Cost of Sales] * [Days Worked]) * (1+vPct_ExternalConsultantCostChange)```
Internal Consultant Cost (What-if)	```sum({<[Employee Type]={'Internal'}>} [Cost of Sales] * [Days Worked]) * (1+vPct_InternalConsultantCostChange)```

 Integrating a global variable into a chart is as easy as treating it as a normal field.

In the input box, if we assign **-35%** to **% External Consultant Cost Change** and **25%** to **% Internal Consultant Cost Change**, we obtain the following result:

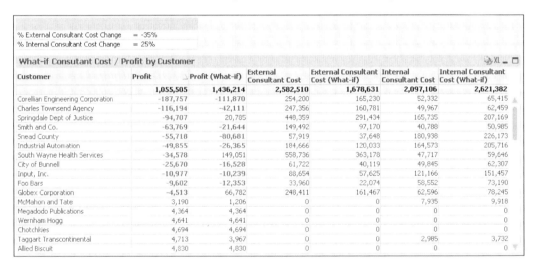

% External Consultant Cost Change = -35%
% Internal Consultant Cost Change = 25%

What-if Consutant Cost / Profit by Customer

Customer	Profit	Profit (What-if)	External Consultant Cost	External Consultant Cost (What-if)	Internal Consultant Cost	Internal Consultant Cost (What-if)
	1,055,505	**1,436,214**	**2,582,510**	**1,678,631**	**2,097,106**	**2,621,382**
Corellian Engineering Corporation	-187,757	-111,870	254,200	165,230	52,332	65,415
Charles Townsend Agency	-116,194	-42,111	247,356	160,781	49,967	62,459
Springdale Dept of Justice	-94,707	20,785	448,359	291,434	165,735	207,169
Smith and Co.	-63,769	-21,644	149,492	97,170	40,788	50,985
Snead County	-55,718	-80,681	57,919	37,648	180,938	226,173
Industrial Automation	-49,855	-26,365	184,666	120,033	164,573	205,716
South Wayne Health Services	-34,578	149,051	558,736	363,178	47,717	59,646
City of Bunnell	-25,670	-16,528	61,722	40,119	49,845	62,307
Input, Inc.	-10,977	-10,239	88,654	57,625	121,166	151,457
Foo Bars	-9,602	-12,353	33,960	22,074	58,552	73,190
Globex Corporation	-4,513	66,782	248,411	161,467	62,596	78,245
McMahon and Tate	3,190	1,206	0	0	7,935	9,918
Megadodo Publications	4,364	4,364	0	0	0	0
Wernham Hogg	4,641	4,641	0	0	0	0
Chotchkies	4,694	4,694	0	0	0	0
Taggart Transcontinental	4,713	3,967	0	0	2,985	3,732
Allied Biscuit	4,830	4,830	0	0	0	0

Samantha can use the preceding what-if analysis to define future objectives that help us to lower the excessive cost of external consultants and generate a profit.

Detailed variable what-if analysis

In some cases, we want to create variables whose values can be changed at a more granular level. For example, Samantha wants to elaborate more on how much the current use of external consultants affects the profit generated from each customer. Since the project requirements are distinctive between customers, she wants to define the days worked by external and internal consultants differently for each customer.

Let's create a chart similar to the previous one, but now incorporating a new field called [Days Worked (What-if)]. We call the chart as **What-if Consultant Days Worked / Cost / Profit by Customer**.

Type of chart	Straight table
Dimension	**Customer**
First metric (Profit)	sum([Profit Margin])
Second metric (Profit (What-if))	sum([Net Sales])- sum({<[Product Type] = {'Licenses','Maintenance'}>} [Cost of Sales])- sum({<[Employee Type]={'External'}>} [Cost of Sales]*[Days Worked (What-if)])- sum({<[Employee Type]={'Internal'}>} [Cost of Sales]*[Days Worked (What-if)])
Third metric (External Consultant Cost)	sum({<[Employee Type]={'External'}>} [Cost of Sales] * [Days Worked])
Fourth metric (External Consultant Cost (What-if))	sum({<[Employee Type]={'External'}>} [Cost of Sales]*[Days Worked (What-if)])
Fifth metric (Internal Consultant Cost)	sum({<[Employee Type]={'Internal'}>} [Cost of Sales] * [Days Worked])
Sixth metric (Internal Consultant Cost (What-if))	sum({<[Employee Type]={'Internal'}>} [Cost of Sales]*[Days Worked (What-if)])

Detailed variables

Our data model has a special field called an **input** field. An input field's values can be changed within any table chart, listbox, or tablebox. Fields that are defined as input fields must be assigned this characteristic at the moment when the data model is created.

Since QlikView cannot compress data in input fields as it compresses read-only data in normal fields, we use this feature with caution on fields that contain more than one million rows of data.

Instead of an input box, we create the following chart to change the values found in [Days Worked (What-if)].

Type of chart	Pivot table
Dimension	**Customer** and **Employee Type**
First metric (Days Worked)	sum([Days Worked])
Second metric (Days Worked (What-if))	InputSum([Days Worked (What-if)])

In addition to applying what we learned in *Chapter 4, Multivariate Analysis*, we select the **Preserve Scroll Position** checkbox in the **Layout** tab, so that we can easily edit the input field's values. We now have the following pivot table:

What-if Consultant Days Worked			XL _ ☐
Customer	**Employee Type**	Days Worked	Days Worked (What-if)
Charles Townsend Agency	⊟ **Total**	**1,747**	**1,747**
	External	820	820
	Internal	927	927
City of Bunnell	⊟ **Total**	**1,474**	**1,474**
	External	289	0
	Internal	1,185	1,474

The input prefix to sum() or avg() will allow us to change the values of an input field within table charts. We change the field's value by clicking the black arrow that appears when hovering over each cell as shown in the following screenshot:

71	71
217	**2,2**◄
24	24

If we modify the subtotal or total, the value is prorated between the rows that make up the subtotal or total. The second parameter of the inputavg() and inputsum() functions defines the type of proration that is applied.

At any time, we can reset an input field's value back to its original state by right-clicking over the chart column that contains `inputsum()`, and selecting any of the three options within **Restore Values**.

After Samantha redistributes all the days worked for our customers of *Corellian Engineering Corporation* and *City of Bunnell,* from external consultants to internal consultants, the values of Days Worked (What-if) are as shown in the following screenshot:

What-if Consultant Days Worked				⚙XL _ ☐
Customer	⚫ **Employee Type**	Days Worked	Days Worked (What-if)	
	⊟ **Total**	**1,474**	**1,474**	▲
City of Bunnell	External	289	0	
	Internal	1,185	1,474	⚫
	⊟ **Total**	**2,404**	**2,404**	
Corellian Engineering Corporation	External	911	0	
	Internal	1,493	2,404	▼

Those new values result in changes to our what-if analysis as shown in the following screenshot:

What-if Consutant Days Worked / Cost / Profit by Customer							⚙XL _ ☐
Customer	Profit	Profit (What-if)	External Consultant Cost	External Consultant Cost (What-if)	Internal Consultant Cost	Internal Consultant Cost (What-if)	
	1,083,211	1,356,152	2,582,510	2,266,587	2,097,106	2,141,195	
Corellian Engineering Corporation	-187,757	34,512	254,200	0	52,332	84,265	▲
Charles Townsend Agency	-116,194	-116,194	247,356	247,356	49,967	49,967	
Springdale Dept of Justice	-94,707	-94,707	448,359	448,359	165,735	165,735	
Smith and Co.	-63,730	-63,730	149,492	149,492	40,788	40,788	
Snead County	-55,718	-55,718	57,919	57,919	180,938	180,938	
Industrial Automation	-49,855	-49,855	184,666	184,666	164,573	164,573	
South Wayne Health Services	-37,660	-37,660	558,736	558,736	47,717	47,717	
City of Bunnell	-25,670	23,896	61,722	0	49,845	62,002	
Input, Inc.	-11,583	-11,583	88,654	88,654	121,166	121,166	
Foo Bars	-9,036	-9,036	33,960	33,960	58,552	58,552	
Globex Corporation	-6,586	-6,586	248,411	248,411	62,596	62,596	
McMahon and Tate	3,167	3,167	0	0	7,935	7,935	
Chotchkies	4,308	4,308	0	0	0	0	
Megadodo Publications	4,364	4,364	0	0	0	0	
Taggart Transcontinental	4,487	4,487	0	0	2,985	2,985	
Wernham Hogg	4,616	4,616	0	0	0	0	
Allied Biscuit	5,364	5,364	0	0	0	0	▼

The yellow backgrounds in the previous table allow us to detect when input values have changed. We implement this feature by adding the following conditional background color to each metric that contains a reference to `sum([Days Worked (What-if)])`.

```
if(
sum([Days Worked (What-if)]) <> sum([Days Worked])
,Yellow(100)
)
```

We can see from this example that by redistributing the days from external consultants to internal consultants, our customers, Corellian Engineering Corporation and City of Bunnell, would have turned a profit.

Summary

What-if analysis is a great final analysis technique. Using the data she supplies, Samantha can test her assumptions based on the historical data and create future objectives that may increase QDataViz, Inc.'s profitability.

After applying this final technique, it's time to bring everything together and communicate the results of our analysis.

9

Dashboards and Navigation

We are now ready to bring everything together and make our case on how to improve QDataViz, Inc. We support our findings with the same charts that we use to visualize and analyze data. If we correctly use the data visualization style guide for each chart, then combining them to tell our story is easy. We create a dashboard as a simple, direct manner to summarize our analysis.

What is a dashboard?

Visual display of the most important information needed to achieve one or more objectives which fits entirely on a single computer screen so it can be monitored at a glance.

— Stephen Few, Dashboard Confusion, Intelligent Enterprise, March 20, 2004

Along with the continual monitoring of information to achieve our objectives, a dashboard helps us to organize and introduce more profound analysis. For example, Samantha wants to create a dashboard which supports her hypothesis that the overuse of external consultants is the cause of QDataViz, Inc.'s problems. If corrective actions are taken, she will continue to use the dashboard to confirm whether her hypothesis is correct.

Our audience may only have a few minutes to review our results. So, unlike previous data visualization techniques that emphasize analysis and discovery, we create dashboards with methods that stress efficient, effective, and summarized communication. We achieve fast and focused knowledge transfer using alerts, mini-graphs, and icons in our dashboard.

The dashboard application

Let's open a new QlikView application to create our sales and project dashboard.

1. Open `Sales_Project_Dashboard.qvw` in the folder `Exercises\Original\`.

2. Change the first sheet's name from **Main** to `Dashboard`.

As in *Chapter 1, First Things First*, we start with a blank QlikView application that contains the customer invoice and project management data model. Our goal is to create the following dashboard during the course of this chapter:

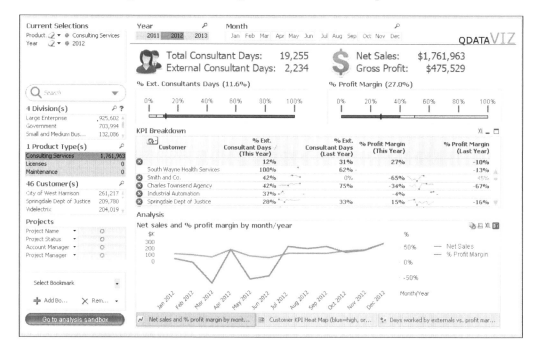

Document settings

First, let's apply a document background that defines our workspace and an object style that minimizes non-data-ink.

1. In the **Settings** menu, click on **Document Properties...**.

2. In the **General** tab, select the **Wallpaper Image** checkbox and click on **Change...**.

3. By default, QlikView installs sample backgrounds and themes. Browse for the folder `C:\Program Files\QlikView\Examples\Developer Toolkit\ backgrounds\with panels` and select `Gray-swirl-White_squared.png`. Click on **OK**.

4. Select **Top** in the **Vertical** drop-down box.

5. Select **Transparent** in the **Sheet Object Style** drop-down box.

6. Click on **OK**.

The new document background outlines a workspace that supports the screen resolution of most tablets (that is, 1024 x 768).

 In a tablet, the empty space along the left and top margins of our dashboard facilitates zooming in and out.

Variables

After experiencing the fast-paced and ever-changing data discovery process in previous chapters, we will look for the ways to create a more stable and easier to maintain QlikView application. Since we often use the same expressions over and over again between separate objects, we store expressions in variables that are maintained in the document's variable repository.

1. In the **Settings** menu, click on **Variable Overview...**.

2. Click on **Add**.

3. Type `vexp_Sales` in the **Variable Name** textbox.

4. Click on **OK**.

5. Select `vexp_Sales` in the **Variables** list.

6. Type `sum([Net Sales])` in the **Definition** textbox.

7. Repeat steps 2 to 6 for the following variables:

Variable name	Definition
vexp_DaysWorked_%ExtConsultant	sum({$<[Employee Type]={'External'}>} [Days Worked]) / sum([Days Worked])
vexp_DaysWorked_%ExtConsultant_ThisYear	sum({$<[Employee Type]={'External'}, Year={$(=max(Year))}>} [Days Worked]) / sum({$<Year={$(=max(Year))}>} [Days Worked])
vexp_DaysWorked_%ExtConsultant_LastYear	sum({$<[Employee Type]={'External'}, Year={$(=max(Year)-1)}>} [Days Worked]) / sum({$<Year={$(=max(Year)-1)}>} [Days Worked])
vexp_%ProfitMargin	sum([Profit Margin])/sum([Net Sales])
vexp_%ProfitMargin_ThisYear	sum({$<Year={$(=max(Year))}>} [Profit Margin]) /sum({$<Year={$(=max(Year))}>} [Net Sales])
vexp_%ProfitMargin_LastYear	sum({$<Year={$(=max(Year)-1)}>} [Profit Margin]) /sum({$<Year={$(=max(Year)-1)}>} [Net Sales])
vexp_Profit	sum([Profit Margin])
vexp_ConsultantsDays	sum([Days Worked])
vexp_ExternalConsultantsDays	sum({$<[Employee Type]={'External'}>} [Days Worked])
vexp_NoConsultants	count(distinct Employee)

8. Click on **OK**.

Instead of explicitly defining a year in set analysis (for example, `Year={2012}`), we define the year dynamically using a dollar sign expansion (for example, `Year={$(=max(Year)-1)}`).

Layout

In most cultures, we are first drawn to review either information located in the top left-hand corner of the screen or information that forms the largest block. We propose the following layout for our dashboard:

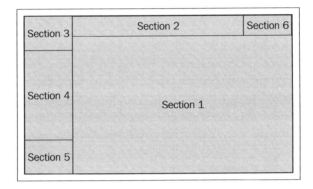

The preceding layout contains the following sections:

- **Section 1**: Area for charts and indicators
- **Section 2**: Date-related filters
- **Section 3**: Current selections
- **Section 4**: Other filters ranked by order of importance or hierarchy
- **Section 5**: Bookmarks and buttons
- **Section 6**: Company logo

Supporting objects

We are going to fill sections 2 to 5 of the preceding layout with the objects that will support the dashboard. Whenever possible, we maintain the same supporting objects in the same location within all the sheets to allow for an efficient and comfortable navigation.

We use lines, text objects, a current selections box, a search object, listboxes, a multibox, and a bookmark object to support our dashboard. We create all of these objects using the design toolbar shown in the following screenshot:

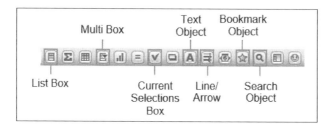

Lines

We use lines along with spacing to divide our proposed dashboard layout into different sections

1. Click on **Create Line/Arrow** in the design toolbar.

2. In the **General** tab, select the **Image** option in the **Background** section and move the slider to the far right to make the object's background transparent.

3. In the **Layout** tab, select the **Bottom** option in the **Layer** section. We can handle up to 99 layers, but assigning the line to the bottom layer is enough to avoid interfering with the manipulation of nearby listboxes that are in the **Normal** layer.

4. In the **Caption** tab, type 230 in the **X-pos** textbox, 55 in the **Y-pos** textbox, and 750 in the **Width** textbox.

5. Click on **OK**.

The line divides the top section of the dashboard layout from the main section. We use spacing alone to divide the left-hand side section from the rest of the dashboard.

Text objects for images

Let's create a text object to add the company logo to the top right-hand corner of the screen, or Section 6 in our proposed dashboard layout.

1. Click on **Create Text Object** in the design toolbar.

2. Select the **Image** option in the **Background** section.

3. Click on **Change** next to the **Image** option.

4. Select QDataViz_Logo.png in the folder Exercises\ Supporting Files\ Images.

5. Click on **OK**.

6. Drag the logo to the top right-hand corner of the screen above the recently created line.

The top part of our dashboard layout should now look similar to the following screenshot:

QDATA VIZ

Current selections box

The current selections box is the most important supporting object in the dashboard. It gives context to the alerts and information we view in the charts. It tells us where we are and prevents us from losing ourselves among the immense combinations of filter selections that are possible.

1. Click on **Create Current Selections Box (C)** in the design toolbar.

2. In the **Caption** tab, clear the **Allow Minimize** checkbox.

3. Click on **OK**.

Drag the current selections box to the top left-hand corner of the screen, or Section 3 of the proposed dashboard layout.

Later, we will resize the current selections box together with rest of the objects located on the left-hand side of the screen.

The search object

Since we have just enough space to put the most pertinent and important information on the dashboard, we cannot create a listbox or multibox for every field. Therefore, we place a search object in the dashboard for any filter selections not covered by the listboxes or multiboxes.

1. Click on **Create Search Object** in the design toolbar.

2. In the **General** tab, select the **Selected Fields** option and add the following fields to the right-hand list **Account Manager, Customer, Customer Country, Customer No., Customer_State, Division, Document No., Document Type, Employee, Employee ID, Employee Position, Employee Type, No. Division, Product Type, Project Code, Project Manager, Project Name,** and **Project Status**.

3. Click on **OK**.

4. Drag the search object to the top left-hand corner of the screen, below the current selections box, or Section 3 of the proposed dashboard layout.

Again, we will resize the search object together with the rest of the objects positioned on the left-hand side of the screen later.

The loaded listboxes

Listboxes are reserved for the most important and commonly used filters. We can also use them for more than just filters and embed key information into the listboxes.

1. Right-click over an empty space in the sheet and click on **Select Fields...**.

2. In the **Fields** tab, add **Customer**, **Division**, and **Product Type** to the **Fields Displayed in Listboxes** list.

3. Click on **OK**.

4. Make the width of all three listboxes similar to the width of the search object and reduce the height of all the listboxes so that only three values are visible in each one.

5. Move the listboxes to Section 4 of the proposed dashboard layout below the search object. The listboxes should be in the following order: **Division**, **Product Type**, and **Customer**.

6. Right-click over the **Division** listbox and select **Properties...**.

7. In the **General** tab, type `=count(distinct Division) & ' Division(s)'` in the **Title** textbox. This adds a dynamic count of the values in the listbox that are selected or related to the selection in another field.

8. In the **Expressions** tab, click on **Add**.

9. In the **Variables** tab of the **Edit Expression** window, select `vexp_Sales` and click on **Paste**.

10. Since the variable contains the text of an expression, we need to pre-evaluate the variable. We use dollar sign expansion, or `$()`, to insert the expression before the metric is calculated. Change the expression from `vexp_Sales` to `$(vexp_Sales)`.

11. We have to manually define the number format of the resulting number, so we use the `num()` function in the final expression.

    ```
    num($(vexp_Sales),'#,##0')
    ```

12. In the **Sort** tab, select the **Expression** checkbox and select **Descending** to the right.

13. Type the expression `$(vexp_Sales)` in the textbox below the **Expression** checkbox.

14. In the **Caption** tab, type `Ordered by net sales` in the **Help Text** textbox. This attribute adds a question mark (**?**) to the caption. We click on or hover over the question mark to show the help text.

15. Click on **OK**.

16. Repeat steps from 6 to 15 for the **Product Type** and **Customer** listboxes.

17. If the text values in the listbox shows an ellipsis (…) at the end, adjust the column width within the listbox. The column boundary is invisible, so move the mouse in between the text value and the net sales amount until the mouse pointer changes into a black bar with opposite arrows ⟷. Once the mouse pointer for column resize appears, adjust the column width appropriately.

We have now created loaded listboxes with a high data density. In the same fashion, we can also add mini-charts to the listboxes.

Important functions

Before moving on to multiboxes, let's take a look at the important functions we just used earlier:

- **&**: The ampersand (`&`) concatenates strings, or text values, together.

- `$(variable)`: We saw dollar sign expansion in *Chapter 3, Trend Analysis*, to precalculate a nested expression. We can also precalculate a variable. In this case, we store the text of an expression in a variable. It is then necessary to pre-evaluate the variable, so that the text is inserted into our metric before it is calculated.

- `num(expression [, format-code [, decimal-sep [, thousands-sep ]]])`: The `num()` function is part of a list of functions that format data. The `date()`, `time()`, `money()`, and `timestamp()` functions format numbers. Each function accepts a second parameter that defines the desired format. In the case of `num()`, an integer is defined using `'#,##0'`.

 More format patterns can be discovered in the **Number** tab of any **Chart Properties** window. Select each number type and review the text in the **Format Pattern** textbox.

Beware of similarly named functions that include the pound sign (#). For example, `num#()` and `date#()` don't return the same result as their format function counterparts. The functions with a pound sign (#) are used to convert text into numbers or dates.

Multibox

Multiboxes are used when we want to add important filters, but have limited space to do so. The best multiboxes have a common theme or hierarchy.

1. Click on **Create Multi Box** in the design toolbar.
2. In the **General** tab, add **Project Name**, **Project Status**, **Account Manager**, and **Project Manager** to the **Fields Displayed in Mutlibox** list.
3. Type `Projects` in the **Title** textbox.
4. Click on **OK**.
5. Drag the multibox to Section 4 of the proposed dashboard layout, below the last listbox.

We will resize all the objects on the left-hand side of the screen after adding a bookmark object.

The bookmark object

Bookmarks save filter selections and views for later consultation. They can even include a comment that adds context to the bookmark.

1. Click on **Create Bookmark Object** in the design toolbar.
2. In the **General** tab, select the **Show Remove Button** checkbox.
3. Click on **OK**.
4. Drag the bookmark object to Section 5 of the proposed dashboard layout, below the multibox.

Arranging objects

The design toolbar contains a series of buttons that help us to arrange and align a group of objects. This part of the design toolbar is shown in the following screenshot:

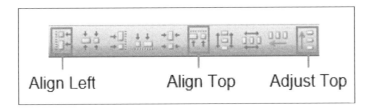

Align Left   Align Top   Adjust Top

1. Holding the *Shift* key, click on each of the objects located in the left-hand side of the screen. Include all the objects from the current selection box down to the bookmark object.

2. Click on **Align Left** in the design toolbar.

3. Click on **Adjust Top** in the design toolbar.

4. If necessary, nudge all the objects a little to the right using the arrow keys. Holding down *Ctrl* while pressing an arrow key will nudge the objects one pixel at a time, and if we need to nudge the objects more, holding down *Ctrl + Shift* will do this ten pixels at a time.

5. Adjust the width of one of the listboxes and notice that most of the objects automatically adjust their width to equal that of the listbox's width.

6. Adjust the width of the multibox and the current selections box by adjusting the column widths within each object first. In the multibox, place the mouse to the left of the black arrow to resize the leftmost column.

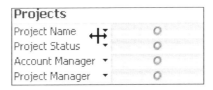

7. The column borders in the current selections box are invisible and can only be adjusted if some selection has been made before. For example, select **Licenses** in the **Product Type** listbox, and then adjust the columns of the current selections object.

8. Finally, adjust the height and width of each object so that together they fit into the workspace defined by the background. Also, avoid overlaping with the horizontal line we created earlier.

Listboxes for dates

The final supporting objects are the date filters located at the top of the dashboard, or in Section 2 of the proposed layout we defined earlier in this chapter.

1. Right-click over the sheet's background and click on **Select Fields**.

2. In the **Fields** tab, add **Month** and **Year** to the **Fields Displayed in Listboxes** list.

3. Click on **OK**.

4. Place the listboxes in the top section of the dashboard to the right of and a little below the current selections box.

5. Right-click over the **Year** listbox and select **Properties**.

6. In the **Presentation** tab, clear the **Single Column** checkbox.

7. Adjust the height and width of the **Year** listbox so that it shows three years in one row.

8. Repeat steps from 5 to 7 for the **Month** listbox.

9. Holding the *Shift* key, select the current selections box along with the **Month** and **Year** listboxes.

10. Click on **Align Top** in the design toolbar.

We now have all the necessary supporting objects in our dashboard as shown in the following screenshot:

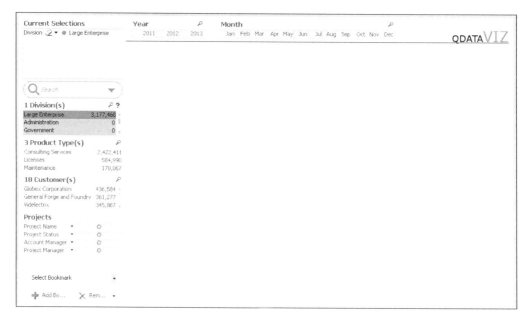

Key Performance Indicators (KPI's)

KPI's are strategically important metrics that are held to be vital for a company's success. Based on our analysis of QDataViz, Inc.'s problems, we've concluded that the excessive use of external consultants has been the cause of the losses incurred in many of our projects. Therefore, we consider the percentage of days worked by external consultants and profit margin to be our KPI's, and aim to monitor their performance with our dashboard.

Icons

We use icons as a graphical identifier of certain subjects. Consistent use of icons can help us link related data and prepare us more rapidly for what to expect. We use text objects to add icons to our dashboard. In the same way we added the company logo in a previous exercise, add the following two icons:

```
Exercises\Supporting Files\Images\Profit.png
```

```
Exercises\Supporting Files\Images\Consultants.png
```

Resize and place the icons below the line as shown in the following screenshot:

Quick global perspective

Before diving into the details, we introduce a global summary that presents an overall picture of the company's situation. We create four textboxes to add this quick global perspective.

1. Click on **Create Text Object** in the design toolbar.

2. In the **General** tab, type the following expression in the **Text** textbox:

    ```
    ='Total Consultant Days: '
    & chr(13) &
    'External Consultant Days: '
    ```

 The chr(13) function forces a line break.

3. Select **Left** in the **Horizontal Alignment** drop-down box.

4. Set the transparency to **100%** in the **Transparency** slider.

5. In the **Font** tab, select **Tahoma** as the **Font** style and **14** as **Font Size**.

6. Click on **OK**.

7. Repeat steps 1 to 6 for the following expression:

```
='Net Sales:'
&chr(13) &
'Gross Profit:'
```

8. Repeat steps 1 to 6 for creating two more textboxes using the following expressions, but instead of aligning the text to the left, align these two textboxes to the right.

Textbox expressions
=num($(vexp_ConsultantsDays),'#,##0') & chr(13) & num($(vexp_ExternalConsultantsDays),'#,##0')
=num($(vexp_Sales),'$#,##0') &chr(13) & num($(vexp_Profit),'$#,##0')

9. Place the four textboxes next to their corresponding icons as shown in the following screenshot:

The gauge chart

Now, let's create two gauge charts that highlight our two KPI's. A gauge chart is represented by the following diagram:

Now lets look at the table which shows the chart specifications:

Type of chart	Gauge chart (refer to the previous diagram)
Dimension	*None*
Metric	`$(vexp_DaysWorked_%ExtConsultant)`

We almost never define a dimension in a gauge chart.
Also, the metric is almost always a ratio.

The default gauge chart is not useful, so we customize it with the following steps in its **Chart Properties** window:

1. In the **General** tab, type the following expression in the **Window Title** textbox.

   ```
   ='% Ext. Consultants Days (' & num
     ($(vexp_DaysWorked_%ExtConsultant) ,'#,##0%') &')'
   ```

2. In the same tab, clear the **Show Title in Chart** checkbox.

3. In the **Style** tab, select the simplified linear gauge (pictured previously) to save space. Also, select the horizontal bar chart in the **Orientation** section.

4. In the **Presentation** tab, clear the **Autowidth Segments** checkbox in the lower left-hand corner of the **Chart Properties** window.

5. Within the **Segments Setup** section, select **Segment 1** in the list of segments and change the color from green to pale green.

6. Select **Segment 2**, type `.05` in the **Lower Bound** textbox and change the color from red to normal yellow.

7. Within the **Segments Setup** section, click on **Add**.

8. Select **Segment 3**, type `.1` in the **Lower Bound** textbox and change the color from green to dark red.

9. Select the **Show Labels on Every Major Unit** checkbox and type `1` in the textbox below it.

10. Select **Line** in the **Style** drop-down box.

11. In the **Number** tab, select the **Integer** option and select the **Show in Percent (%)** checkbox.

12. Click on **OK**.

13. Resize the chart so it looks like the following chart:

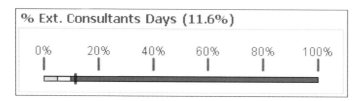

We repeat the same exercise as mentioned earlier for the percentage profit margin KPI. For this gauge chart, the metric is `vexp_%ProftiMargin` and the segments are defined as follows:

Segment	Lower Bound	Color
Segment 1	0	Dark red
Segment 2	.4	Yellow
Segment 3	.5	Pale green

We place the two gauge charts below their corresponding icon as shown in the following screenshot:

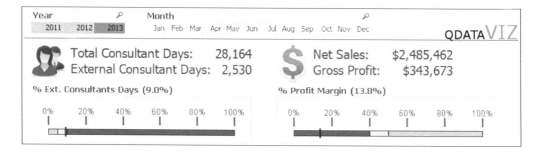

KPI breakdown

After reviewing QDataViz, Inc.'s global external consultant usage and profit margin, we breakdown the KPI's by product type, division, and customer.

The KPI table

Let's create a table chart that contains time period comparisons, alerts, and mini-charts.

Type of chart	Straight table chart
Dimension	clKPI (a cyclical dimensional group we create that contains **Customer**, **Division**, and **Product Type**)
Metrics	$(vexp_DaysWorked_%ExtConsultant_ThisYear) $(vexp_DaysWorked_%ExtConsultant_LastYear) $(vexp_%ProfitMargin_ThisYear) $(vexp_%ProfitMargin_LastYear)

We apply the rules defined in the data visualization style guide for table charts found in *Chapter 4*, *Multivariate Analysis*, and obtain the following table as a result:

Customer	% Ext. Consultant Days (This Year)	% Ext. Consultant Days (Last Year)	% Profit Margin (This Year)	% Profit Margin (Last Year)
	12%	31%	27%	-10%
Smith and Co.	42%	0%	-65%	45%
Taggart Transcontinental	0% -		-53% -	
General Forge and Foundry	8%	8%	-51%	24%
Charles Townsend Agency	42%	75%	-34%	-67%
Foo Bars	10%	2%	-33%	22%
Input, Inc.	10%	0%	-7%	62%

KPI Breakdown

We add visual cues to the table chart to help our minds to rapidly detect patterns.

Visual cues

When we use three or less colors, we use visual cues instead of modifying the expression's background color.

1. Right-click on the chart object and select **Properties...**.

2. In the **Visual Cues** tab, select % **Ext. Consultant Days (This Year)** and % **Ext. Consultant Days (Last Year)** in the **Expressions** list.

3. Type .1 in the **Upper** textbox, change the text color to **Red** and select the **Bold** checkbox.

4. Change the normal text color to **Orange**.

5. Type .05 in the **Lower** textbox and change the text color to **Blue**.

6. In the **Visual Cues** tab, select % **Profit Margin (This Year)** and % **Profit Margin (Last Year)** in the **Expressions** list.

7. Type .5 in the **Upper** textbox and change the text color to **Blue**.

8. Change the normal text color to **Orange**.

9. Type .4 in the **Lower** textbox, change the text color to **Red** and select the **Bold** checkbox.

10. Click on **OK**.

Alert images

For more complex and custom alerts, we can use an if-statement and images.

1. Right-click on the chart object and select **Properties...**.

2. In the **Expression** tab, click on **Add.**

3. In the **Edit Expression** window, type the following incomplete expression:

```
if([% Profit Margin (This Year)] < .4 and [% Ext.
  Consultant Days (This Year)] > .1,
```

4. Place the cursor at the end of the incomplete expression and click the **Images** tab at the bottom of the **Edit Expression** window.

5. Click on **Advanced...**.

6. Select the red circle with a cross.

7. Click on **Paste**.

8. Finish the expression with the following text:

```
,'')
```

9. Confirm that the expression appears as follows:

```
if([% Profit Margin (This Year)] < .4 and [% Ext. Consultant Days
(This Year)] > .1,
'qmem://<bundled>/BuiltIn/cross_r.png','')
```

10. Click on **OK**.

11. Select the new expression and leave a blank space in the **Label** textbox. This causes the label to be blank.

12. In the **Expression** tab, select **Image** in the **Representation** drop-down box.

13. Select **Keep Aspect** in the **Image Formatting** drop-down box.

14. Click on **OK**.

The mini-charts

We take advantage of the limited space in the dashboard to add mini-charts to the KPI breakdown table chart just as we did in *Chapter 4, Multivariate Analysis*.

So far we have the following dashboard:

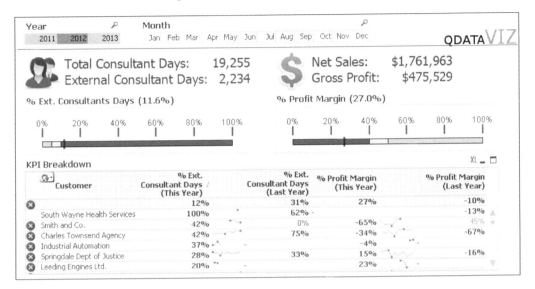

Brief analysis

We support our argument and allow for some analysis to be done in the dashboard by adding certain charts from `Sales_Project_Analysis_Sandbox.qvw`.

1. Open `Sales_Project_Analysis_Sandbox.qvw`

2. Copy each of the following charts and paste them into the `Sales_Project_Dashboard.qvw`.

   ○ Net sales and % profit margin by month/year (refer to *Chapter 3, Trend Analysis*)

   ○ Customer KPI heat map (refer to *Chapter 4, Multivariate Analysis*)

   ○ Days worked by externals vs. profit margin by project (refer to *Chapter 6, Correlation Analysis*)

Migration

We should consider a few migration issues when we copy charts from one application to another.

1. In the **Settings** menu, click on **Expression Overview**.

2. Select all five checkboxes in the upper left-hand corner of the **Expression Overview** window to view all the available expressions types.

3. Click on **Find/Replace**.

4. Clear the **In Selection** checkbox and the **Case Sensitive** checkbox.

5. Type Sum([Net Sales]) in the **Find What** textbox and $(vexp_Sales) in the **Replace With** textbox.

6. Click on **Replace All**.

7. Repeat steps 5 and 6 for the following texts:

Find what	Replace with
sum([Days Worked])	$(vexp_ConsultantsDays)
sum([Profit Margin])/sum([Net Sales])	$(vexp_%ProfitMargin)
sum([Profit Margin])	$(vexp_Profit)
count(distinct Employee)	$(vexp_NoConsultants)
sum({$<[Employee Type] = {'External'}>} [Days Worked])	$(vexp_ExternalConsultantsDays)

The container object

We use a container object to organize the charts used for analysis in the dashboard.

1. Click on **Create Container** 🔲 in the design toolbar.

2. In the **General** tab, select the three charts that we just added to the dashboard and click on **Add >**.

3. In the **Presentation** tab, select **Tabs at bottom** in the **Appearance** drop-down box.

4. In the **Caption** tab, type Analysis in the **Title Text** textbox.

5. Click on **OK**.

We notice that while we have a new container object that includes our analytical charts, we still possess the lone analytical charts outside the container. Select the lone analytical charts and delete them.

When we delete the charts we are warned that the object is linked to other objects. In this case, the lone chart is linked to the same chart in the container. Click on **Delete Selected** to maintain the copy that is located in the container.

Adjust the size of the container object and place it with KPI breakdown.

Buttons and actions

If it is necessary to perform detailed analysis, we create a link to the sandbox application.

1. Click on **Create Button** 🔲 in the design toolbar.

2. In the **General** tab, type `Go to analysis sandbox` in the **Text** textbox.

3. In the **Actions** tab, click on **Add**.

4. Select **External** in the **Action Type** list and **Open QlikView Document** in the **Action** list. Click on **OK**.

5. In the **Document** textbox, type `Sales_Project_Analysis_Sandbox.qvw` if the sandbox application shares the same folder as `Sales_Project_Dashboard.qvw`. Otherwise, include the file path where the sandbox application is found. For example, `C:\QlikView\Sales_Project_Analysis_Sandbox.qvw`.

6. Select the **Transfer State** checkbox.

7. Click on **OK**.

8. Adjust the size of the button and place it below the bookmark object.

9. Click on the button and confirm that `Sales_Project_Analysis_Sandbox.qvw` opens with the filter selections included in `Sales_Project_Dashboard.qvw`.

We now have a completed dashboard, which Samantha can use for her final presentation and continual follow-up of the key performance indicators, as shown in the following screenshot:

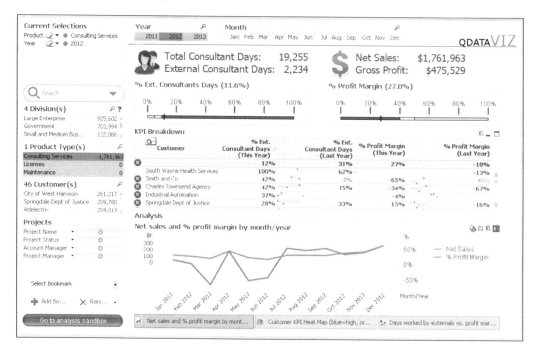

Summary

We have now concluded our project at QDataViz, Inc. We combined the analysis that we've described in the previous chapters to create a dashboard, which is used to present a possible cause of the company's losses and continually monitor the key performance indicators that resulted from our analysis. In time, we expect that our hypothesis will be proven true, and as the participation of external consultants decreases, our profit margins will increase.

Most importantly, we have given Samantha the ability to continue and solve other problems. She still has much more to learn about data visualization and QlikView, but she now knows enough to tackle numerous analytical challenges. Samantha might not remember every rule of the data visualization style guide, but she does recognize the fundamental reasoning behind the rules that allow for effective and efficient analysis and communication.

Now it's time to start your own data visualization adventure. What will you discover?

Index

Symbols

$() function 42

A

additional expressions
  about 28
  Set Analysis 29, 30
additional metric, line chart 45
adequate labeling
  axes label 22
  dimension label 21, 22
  metric label 21, 22
  using 21
Aggregation drop-down box 18
Aggr() function 57
alert images 126
area map chart
  about 94
  data visualization style guide, rules 96
  dimension 95
  metric 95, 96
ARGB() function 42
associative data model 10
Available Fields/Groups list 18, 27, 28
Average mode 78
axes labels 38, 39
Axes tab 23, 34

B

bar chart
  about 18
  modifying 19, 20
  screenshot 19
  using, for rank analysis 18

Bar Chart checkbox 32
bar chart manipulation
  chart width to height ratio 33
  Force 0 checkbox, clearing 34
bar charts
  data visualization style guide 21
  supported objects 20
bar charts labeling
  and line charts, differences 38
Before Reload checkbox 11
bookmark object 118
Box plot 77
Box Plot Wizard 77

C

caption
  Copy Image to Clipboard 32
  exporting, to Excel 32
  graphs, changing 32
  icons 47
  maximize 32
  minimize 32
Caption tab 21, 32, 33, 98
chartjunk
  axis, throwing 46
  grid lines, throwing 46
Chart label 38
Chart Properties window 33
chr() function 42
Color Expression text box 96
coloring technique, bar chart
  associative 23, 24
  highlighting 24, 25
Colors tab 24
concat() function 42

Thank you for buying
Learning QlikView Data Visualization

About Packt Publishing

Packt, pronounced 'packed', published its first book "Mastering phpMyAdmin for Effective MySQL Management" in April 2004 and subsequently continued to specialize in publishing highly focused books on specific technologies and solutions.

Our books and publications share the experiences of your fellow IT professionals in adapting and customizing today's systems, applications, and frameworks. Our solution based books give you the knowledge and power to customize the software and technologies you're using to get the job done. Packt books are more specific and less general than the IT books you have seen in the past. Our unique business model allows us to bring you more focused information, giving you more of what you need to know, and less of what you don't.

Packt is a modern, yet unique publishing company, which focuses on producing quality, cutting-edge books for communities of developers, administrators, and newbies alike. For more information, please visit our website: www.packtpub.com.

About Packt Enterprise

In 2010, Packt launched two new brands, Packt Enterprise and Packt Open Source, in order to continue its focus on specialization. This book is part of the Packt Enterprise brand, home to books published on enterprise software – software created by major vendors, including (but not limited to) IBM, Microsoft and Oracle, often for use in other corporations. Its titles will offer information relevant to a range of users of this software, including administrators, developers, architects, and end users.

Writing for Packt

We welcome all inquiries from people who are interested in authoring. Book proposals should be sent to author@packtpub.com. If your book idea is still at an early stage and you would like to discuss it first before writing a formal book proposal, contact us; one of our commissioning editors will get in touch with you.

We're not just looking for published authors; if you have strong technical skills but no writing experience, our experienced editors can help you develop a writing career, or simply get some additional reward for your expertise.

QlikView 11 for Developers

ISBN: 978-1-84968-606-8   Paperback: 534 pages

Develop Business Intelligence applications with QlikView 11

1. Learn to build applications for Business Intelligence while following a practical case -- HighCloud Airlines. Each chapter develops parts of the application and it evolves throughout the book along with your own QlikView skills.

2. The code bundle for each chapter can be accessed on your local machine without having to purchase a QlikView license.

3. The hands-on approach allows you to build a QlikView application that integrates real data from several different sources and presents it in dashboards, analyses and reports.

Instant QlikView 11 Application Development

ISBN: 978-1-84968-964-9   Paperback: 60 pages

An intuitive guide to building and customizing a business intelligence application for your data

1. Learn something new in an Instant! A short, fast, focused guide delivering immediate results

2. Learn how to analyze data for business discovery with QlikView 11 with automatic data linking and wizards

3. Create your own analysis interfaces using tables, lists, and charts

Please check **www.PacktPub.com** for information on our titles

QlikView for Developers Cookbook

ISBN: 978-1-78217-973-3   Paperback: 290 pages

Discover the strategies needed to tackle the most challenging tasks facing the QlikView developer

1. Learn beyond QlikView training

2. Discover QlikView Advanced GUI development, advanced scripting, complex data modelling issues, and much more

3. Accelerate the growth of your QlikView developer ability

4. Based on over 7 years' experience of QlikView development

Tableau Data Visualization Cookbook

ISBN: 978-1-84968-978-6   Paperback: 172 pages

Over 70 recipes for creating visual stories with your data using Tableau

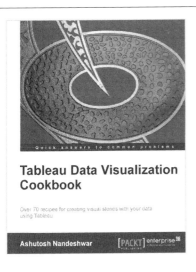

1. Quickly create impressive and effective graphics which would usually take hours in other tools

2. Lots of illustrations to keep you on track

3. Includes examples that apply to a general audience

Please check **www.PacktPub.com** for information on our titles

11491648R00089

Made in the USA
San Bernardino, CA
18 May 2014